1970

ok may be kept

AN INTRODUCTION TO
VIRGIL'S AENEID

AN INTRODUCTION TO
VIRGIL'S AENEID

W. A. CAMPS

OXFORD UNIVERSITY PRESS
1969

Oxford University Press, Ely House, London W.1

GLASGOW NEW YORK TORONTO MELBOURNE WELLINGTON
CAPE TOWN SALISBURY IBADAN NAIROBI LUSAKA ADDIS ABABA
BOMBAY CALCUTTA MADRAS KARACHI LAHORE DACCA
KUALA LUMPUR SINGAPORE HONG KONG TOKYO

PRINTED IN GREAT BRITAIN
BY BUTLER AND TANNER LTD
FROME AND LONDON

PREFACE

This book is addressed to students of Latin and of literature in general, including those who are approaching Virgil for the first time; it contains little that can be new to the professional Virgilian scholar, and a great deal that will be too familiar to merit his attention. It is of course heavily indebted to the work of other writers on Virgil, past and present. It represents, as any book on Virgil will inevitably do, a personal view rather than one universally agreed, but includes (I hope) enough factual information to prevent its usefulness depending too much on the value of the author's opinions. It attempts to cover all the more important aspects of the poem which is its subject, but in an illustrative manner only, with the hope of helping the reader but not of doing for him what he may find more interest in doing for himself.

The general plan is as follows. Chapters II–V discuss the subject of the *Aeneid*, the story of the principal characters, and the dominant features of the background against which these play out their parts. Chapters V–VI discuss the poet's arts of construction and expression. Chapters VIII–XI treat of the materials from history and literature on which Virgil has drawn in making the fabric of his narrative and the associations which it evokes in consequence. The first chapter deals with considerations which it is useful to have in mind in reading the poem, anticipating in the process some elements of what is said later; but the reader not yet well acquainted with the content of the poem may find it best to postpone this at a first reading and begin with Chapter II. This chapter and the following Chapters, III and IV, include summary accounts of the story as a whole and of certain themes within it, partly for the benefit of the newcomer to the *Aeneid*, but partly also because a summary narrative of this kind may be the most economical way of conveying an interpretation. The appendices which follow at the end of the book are, naturally enough, a miscellany. Some are designed to give the student an outline of information about subsidiary matters which he may otherwise find mysterious when he encounters incidental references to them elsewhere. Some contain matter which seemed possibly important but which did not fit into the ordinary pattern of the book.

Sir Roger Mynors, Mr. L. P. Wilkinson and Mr. J. A. F. Yudkin have helped me with criticisms and suggestions which I gratefully acknowledge; but they bear no responsibility for whatever faults are in this book as it now stands. I want to thank also the members of a class at University College, Toronto, in the autumn term of 1966, and pupils at Cambridge over a number of years.

W. A. C.

Cambridge
  [*December 1968*]

CONTENTS

APPENDICES (CONT.)

OTHER READING

Notable books and essays on Virgil have appeared in recent years, and a review of these, together with a guide to bibliographies of older Virgilian scholarship and criticism, has been given by R. D. Williams in a recent pamphlet, *Virgil* (1967), in the series called *New Surveys in the Classics.** In view of this, I will mention here only a very few short works which offer particular advantages to the non-specialist reader, but which for one reason or another might easily escape his notice. Tarn and Charlesworth's *Octavian, Antony and Cleopatra* (reprinted in 1965 from the *Cambridge Ancient History*) gives an excellent account of the historical events which were fresh in memory at the time when the *Aeneid* was written. Chapters 5–8 of C. S. Lewis's Preface to *Paradise Lost* (1942) and Chapters 4–5 of E. M. W. Tillyard's *English Epic and its Background* (1964) give the views on the *Aeneid* of two men who were educated in the classical curriculum but spent their working lives as students and critics of English literature. Dryden's *Dedication* prefixed to his translation of the *Aeneid* gives the comments of one major poet on another in the light of the close acquaintance that only the effort of translation can impart; though in reading it one must be prepared to make allowance for great differences between the academic and social conditions of Dryden's world and ours. Lastly, it would be a pity if H. Nettleship's *Suggestions Introductory to a Study of the Aeneid* (in *Lectures and Essays*; 1895) should cease to be noticed; for it says a great deal in a small space, and documents what it says with valuable annotations. In recommending these books I do not mean to imply that the opinions they express agree in every instance with my own.

* Published in the first instance as supplements to *Greece & Rome*, and thereafter available either through booksellers or direct from the Joint Association of Classical Teachers at the Classical Association.

I

PRELIMINARY

THE poet of the *Aeneid* was born in the year 70 B.C. in what was then Cisalpine Gaul, and composed the *Aeneid* in the last ten or eleven years of his life. He died in 19 B.C. These dates are of significance for two reasons. First, because they set the poem in its broad historical perspective, at the beginning of the Roman Empire's long existence as a relatively stable and peaceful unit of government, near to the beginning of the Christian era, and at the zenith of Greco-Roman literary culture. Secondly, because the actual events of Virgil's lifetime are very relevant to the content of his poem. It was only during that lifetime that the people of his own homeland became Italians and Roman citizens, and only in the previous generation that Roman citizenship had been extended to the Italian peoples south of the Po. Hence it is a result of a development still recent, when Virgil wrote, that the Rome to which the *Aeneid* looks forward is not the mistress of Italy but its capital and the common pride and property of the Italian race. But more important still is the fact that Virgil was twenty-one when the civil wars of Rome began with Caesar's crossing of the Rubicon, and forty when they ended with the defeat and death of Mark Antony at Alexandria in the year 30 B.C. Thus the first twenty years of Virgil's adult life were passed under the shadow of the civil war, and the *Aeneid* was written in the decade immediately following the restoration of peace and order. The emotions of this time are expressed in the *Aeneid* in three great prophetic passages, and the realization in tranquillity of the greatness of Rome's achievement and the hopes of a new era founded on it are the inspiration behind the poem and provide one of its dominant themes.[1] Another is provided by the poet's awareness of the cost paid by Romans and others in the process which had made Rome great.

The restoration of peace and promise of a new era is associated in the prophetic passages mentioned with the person of Caesar's heir Octavian (Augustus),* and there is more than one reminder in the

Note. Most of the references and notes are grouped at the end of the book; they are indicated in the text by numbers. But a few of more general interest are printed as footnotes; they are indicated by * and †.

* Octavian's mother, Atia, was a niece of Julius Caesar; and Caesar adopted him, in his will, as son.

poem that its hero Aeneas is ancestor of Octavian through the supposed descent of the Julii from Aeneas' son Iulus. It is indeed clear
that the figure of Aeneas is intended at times to evoke Octavian; and
it is possible that it is substantially modelled on Virgil's conception
of Octavian's character, for the picture is singular enough to suggest
that a real model is at the back of it—a man burdened by responsibility, sustaining his role by a prolonged exertion of the will, inspired
and upheld by the memory of his father, humane by nature but
capable of cruelty in avenging one he loved, ruthless in pursuit of
what he sees as his duty and endowed with extraordinary personal
magnetism.[2] Whether Octavian was such a man we cannot now
know; but it would not be surprising that Virgil should see him so;
and it will be observed that the picture is not a simple idealization.
We do know that Virgil enjoyed the patronage, and indeed the
friendship of the emperor and of his minister Maecenas, and that he
was endowed with a comfortable fortune by them and other
admirers.[3] We also know that Octavian and Maecenas were concerned to encourage Latin letters as part of the cultural and moral
revival of Rome in the new era, and that a Latin epic worthy to be
set beside the poems of Homer was especially desired. But nothing
known to us authorizes the supposition that the Aeneid was written
by command, or that the sentiments animating it were not those of
Virgil himself. There was every reason why he should admire the
splendour of Rome's achievement, and every reason why he should
be glad and grateful for the ending of the civil wars; every reason
also why he should wish (though with diffidence, we know)* to
fulfil the gift of poetry which he knew he possessed in the poetic form
which to the mind of his age was incomparably the best, and to
serve his country in so doing as others served it in other spheres. But
the *Aeneid* is in no sense political propaganda, for it is not in its
nature a political poem. The Rome that is its inspiration is not conceived in terms of a political system; and the background against
which the humans in the story act and suffer is provided not by contrasting political ideas but by the working of the historical process
and the conflict of spiritual powers.

Before the *Aeneid* Virgil had produced two major works, the
Eclogues and the *Georgics*. The first is a collection of ten short pieces
(from 63 to 111 lines) forming a Latin counterpart, with important

---

* In a letter to Augustus while he was working on the *Aeneid* he said that he felt
he must have been 'almost out of his mind' when he embarked on it (Macrobius
1.24.10–11).

differences, to the pastoral idylls of Theocritus. The second is a collection of four discourses of rather more than 500 lines apiece on four departments of agriculture, developing the theme of the *Works and Days* of Hesiod, but covering a wider range, and belonging rather to a genre of didactic poetry favoured in the Hellenistic age, though essentially different in spirit again from that.* In the series formed by these and the *Aeneid* together various patterns of literary procedure can be observed. For instance, an ascent in terms of poetic levels is apparent; from the supposedly rustic simplicity of the pastoral first to the dignity of didactic (certified by the prestige of Hesiod) and then to the most exalted and consequently most exacting of all kinds of poetry, the epic. Or again, there is the evident intention in each case to produce a Latin counterpart (though not a mere imitation) of an acknowledged masterpiece of Greek literature: Virgil becomes successively the Roman Theocritus, the Roman Hesiod, and finally the Roman Homer. Or again, the same process can be seen as the Latin development of the Hellenistic development of an early Greek form: thus the Greek mime passes through Theocritus' pastoral version to Virgil and emerges as the *Eclogues*, the primitive didactic of Hesiod passes through the sophisticated didactic of the Hellenistic age to become the *Georgics*, the primary epic of Homer passes through the aetiological and episodic treatment of legend by the Hellenistics to become (with a difference) the *Aeneid*. For the *Aeneid* is in one sense a collection of splendid episodes; and in another sense it is an *aition* (the legendary or mythical origin of an existing something, a subject of poetry much affected by the Greek poets of the Hellenistic age) of nothing else but Rome itself. But more important than these fancies for the understanding of the *Aeneid* are the anticipations in the *Eclogues* and *Georgics* of certain distinctive features of Virgilian method—the systematic organization of the material, the kaleidoscopic rearrangement of words and motifs taken from a predecessor (respectfully) to make something wholly

---

* By 'Hellenistic age' is here meant the three centuries of Greek history following the death of Alexander the Great in 323 B.C.; in which Greek became the *lingua franca* of the eastern Mediterranean, and the Greek monarchies established by Alexander's marshals in lands whose peoples were not Greek by race became centres of a new kind of Greek culture. The Greek poetry of this age is called sometimes 'Hellenistic', but more often 'Alexandrian', because the most vigorous cultural centre was Alexandria, and poets and scholars congregated there from other parts of the Greek world; many important literary figures of the period were however not associated with Alexandria. A summary account of the varieties of poetry characteristic of this period will be found in E. A. Barber's article 'Alexandrian Poetry' in the *Oxford Classical Dictionary*.

new, the expression of essential feelings through strands of sentiment running through a mass of apparently disparate material, and elements of determinable symbolism and indeterminate suggestiveness equally pervasive of the whole—though operating usually so as to extend the significance of the material outwardly rather than as an essential cause of its inward cohesion.

Stories were current in the ancient world about Virgil's method of working.[4] There is no way of proving that these were true and not simply fables of the kind that accumulate readily about a famous name. But they are circumstantial, undramatic, intrinsically plausible, and in harmony with the facts as we can observe them in the poem itself. We are told that the *Aeneid* was complete in substance when the poet died, but unfinished in the sense of lacking final revision; and that this process of revision was to be so extensive that the poet had set aside three whole years for it. We are told further that Virgil made a plan of the whole story in prose before beginning to make the poem as such; and that he then composed the poetic version section by section, not necessarily following the order of the story: that is to say, passages which we now find in the earlier books may in some cases have been composed later than passages which we find in the later books. We are not told how full was the prose outline—whether a brief sketch like the outlines Milton drew up for the drama that was never written and was superseded by *Paradise Lost*,[5] or a complete prose narrative, or (as seems most likely) something between the two, a fairly full précis of the whole story, subject no doubt to modification as the work proceeded. As regards the making of the poetry itself, it is reported (specifically of the *Georgics*, but there is no reason to think that what is said of them is not true of the *Aeneid* also) that Virgil's practice was to dictate a considerable passage in the morning and then spend the rest of the day in selection and re-working of this material, until perhaps the final product consisted of only a few lines. Speaking of this the poet himself used to say, we are informed, that he produced his poetry 'as a she-bear does her cubs', beginning with portions of roughly formed material and licking it gradually into its proper shape. It accords with this that he is said also to have left some passages still in a rough state, or imperfectly fitted into their context, and to have made do in various places with makeshift verses 'so as not to interrupt the flow of his inspiration'.[6]

These reports about Virgil's way of working seem, as has already been said, to be confirmed by the evidence of the poem, and also by

what we hear of the practice of other writers. There are intricacies
in the construction of the *Aeneid* which imply a carefully elaborated
initial plan, rather than a spontaneously developing sequence of
events.[7] And that the building of the poem on this initial framework
did not proceed in a logical or chronological sequence seems to be
shown by internal discrepancies, such as the introduction of Nisus
and Euryalus as new characters in Book 9 when as the poem now
stands they have already made a conspicuous appearance in Book 5.
The dictation of considerable passages of verse, after reflection no
doubt but with a spontaneity of 'flow', would not in itself be unusual
in that world: Ovid testifies himself to his own fluency as a com-
poser, and Cicero says of the poet Archias that this client of his
could produce impromptu any number of 'excellent verses' without
benefit of pen and paper.[8] This dictation was of course in Virgil's case
only the first stage. But in fact there have survived in the poem a
number of lines whose flabby phrasing seems to mark them as
metrical props or makeshifts, as well as a number of lines that are
metrically incomplete.[9] We are reminded here that the *Aeneid* in the
state in which Virgil left it at his death had still three whole years of
work to be done upon it.

If at one stage of the composition of individual passages the poet
was letting his words flow with a certain spontaneous continuity, a
likely consequence would be that phrases or images which he had
adopted in one context would come to his mind in the making of
another, because this tendency is inherent in the process of rapid
composition. Sometimes the associations of the earlier passage
(earlier in order of composition, but not necessarily in its position in
the poem) may be relevant to the new context; but often this will not
be the case, and the words will have come to mind simply because
the requirements of the new context invite them.[10] This in fact can be
observed to happen very frequently in the *Aeneid*, and it is important
not to expect in such repetitions a significance which does not
usually attach to them.

If the poet's method of working concentrated his mind, in the act
of composition, on the individual episode, and in developing the
episode yielded to the immediate impulse of his imagination, a
likely result would be the occurrence of minor discrepancies of fact
between passages composed at different times and in different parts
of the poem, because each scene as it develops under the immediate
impulse of the imagination may develop away from the concept
which prevailed elsewhere. Such discrepancies are in fact found in

a number of places in the *Aeneid*, and in so far as they are not trivial they would no doubt have been detected and removed in the finishing process which Virgil did not live to complete.[11]

The traditional account of Virgil's method—of the combination of a carefully organized original design of the whole with a strong focusing of the imagination on the individual episode in the act of poetic composition—thus accords with the impression of a certain incoherence of detail within a strongly systematized framework which the poem leaves upon many readers. It may also explain (though other explanations are possible) a certain lack of explicitness about the relevance of particular episodes to the psychology of characters who appear extensively in the poem—that is to say, the hero Aeneas and the secondary hero Turnus who is opposed to him through all the second half of the story. This lack of explicitness is not necessarily a fault; and it happens with any work of literature, and especially with the drama, that different readers or expositors may interpret the same character in widely different ways, by different understanding of ambiguities in the author's text, by emphasizing what others leave unemphasized and vice versa, and by imposing constructions where the author has not evidently imposed them (though they may none the less correspond to his intention). Some examples may help to illustrate this point as it applies to the *Aeneid*. The hero's moment of weakness at Carthage comes immediately after his father's death, and is followed, after his flight from that temptation, by events (in Books 5 and 6) which emphatically evoke his father's memory and the bond between father and son and the inspiration the son draws from the father in the pursuit of his mission. Accordingly, some readers see Aeneas at Carthage as rendered emotionally vulnerable by the loss he has so recently sustained. Virgil nowhere says or implies that this is so, and we cannot tell whether he thought in such terms in this context. But the construction is perhaps legitimate for a modern reader. Again, Turnus in the tenth book of the poem is removed, involuntarily, from the battlefield, and so leaves his men to fight without him. Some readers feel that the sense of anger with himself that a man of his character will experience on this account is background to the violence of his anger with others later. It may be that the poet so conceives the situation; but if so he has given no indication of it in the text. A similar question arises, with more important consequences, in connection with the hero's descent into the underworld in the sixth book. Up to this point in the story he has appeared often to be hesitant or disheartened; in what follows he is unhesitant and confident at all times. Hence the experience of the sixth book is interpreted by many readers as a formative spiritual experience, from which the hero emerges purged of his earlier weakness and re-born as a new man, having learned no longer to look back with nostalgia to the past but to look forward with hope to the future.[12] But Virgil nowhere says anything to suggest that this is his conception of the matter; and if it were, one might expect that he would lay some emphasis on an idea so striking and so rich in significance. What he says at the time is that Aeneas is fired with hope of the glory that is promised him (in the vision of future leaders of his nation which is a part, and a part only, of the experience he has gone through);[13] nothing is said of regeneration or of liberation from the past. And the change in the hero's demeanour in the books that follow is sufficiently explained by the fact that in the scene next following the descent to the underworld he reaches the end of his quest and knows that he has found at last the new homeland for which he has hitherto been searching in uncertainty and tribulation; he also receives in confirmation of this a whole succession of supernatural assurances and promises of victory in the battle which lies ahead.[14] It will be seen from this and the previous examples that for a commentator at least it is often necessary to make a distinction between what Virgil says and what he seems to a given reader to imply; about the former there can be agreement, but the latter depends to a great extent on the subjective response of the individual reader. For the individual reader, as opposed to the commentator, it may be right to yield himself to this subjective response, however personal, because the power to evoke such response, often highly personal, is a peculiar virtue of Virgil's poetry.

A similar reserve on the part of the commentator and freedom of personal response on the part of the individual reader commends itself also in regard to the evocative symbolism (let us say, for want of a less ambiguous word) in which the *Aeneid* abounds. The concept of a saviour god who 'came in the fulness of time in answer to our yearning'[15] has particular associations for a reader in the Christian era which he cannot escape, and which yet can have had no place in the mind of Virgil. The thought that the flames of Dido's pyre which Aeneas sees as he looks back over the sea to Carthage[16] anticipate the flames with which his descendants in history are to destroy Dido's city is one that the poet may have shared with modern readers to whom it comes; but we cannot tell whether this was so. On the other hand, we also cannot tell how often associations that were full of significance for Virgil and his readers are lost to us because of our comparative ignorance of the contemporary background. Early in the first book of the Aeneid is a scene in which a violent tempest provoked by malevolent powers is miraculously subdued by the god Neptune, whom the poet then displays riding in his chariot over the resulting expanse of calm. This manifestation of the god would evoke for Virgil's contemporaries the thought of Octavian Caesar, restorer of peace after the civil wars, for the reason that he was commonly depicted in contemporary works of art in the style and role of Neptune here described;[17] but had not examples of these representations happened to survive, this particular evocative value of the scene would be lost for us, and we have no means of knowing how much of the same kind we are missing elsewhere. It will be noticed further that 'symbolism' works in the poem in a variety of different ways that cross with one another. Thus a figure in the poem may suggest by some resemblance a figure in history outside it, as Dido by resemblance suggests (in some respects) Cleopatra or Aeneas suggests (in some respects) Octavian. Or a figure in the poem may typify a nation or a quality, as Dido stands (in one sense) for Carthage and Aeneas stands (in one sense) for the Roman values of *pietas* and *virtus* which he embodies. Or an event may be a physical manifestation of something in the moral sphere, as the storm at the beginning of the poem is a symptom and so an expression of the rage of Juno against the Trojans. Or an object may be felt to possess a significance which remains unidentifiable, and for this very reason to invest with a quality of romantic mystery the scene in which it is set—as for instance the Golden Bough. It results from this variety of kinds of evocative correspondence that the same thing or person may be significant of more things than one: as Dido evokes both Carthage and Cleopatra, and Aeneas stands both for Octavian and for the Roman traditions which he embodies—and this statement does not of course exhaust the representative significance of either figure. Conversely different figures within the poem may in their several contexts have a symbolic reference to the same figure outside it, as the gods Neptune and Hercules and the hero Aeneas all in their different ways evoke aspects of Octavian.[18] It is thus unlikely that systematic patterns of symbolism should be expected in the *Aeneid*, and likely that what sometimes begin to appear as such are due (with limited exceptions which will appear later) simply to the way in which Virgil's creative imagination works, echoing history and contemporary experience as well as literary precedents in the process of making his story and finding the language in which to clothe it. The result is an accompaniment of associations which enriches his narrative but does not substitute a new meaning for the meaning which it outwardly bears. Thus, the whole story is in a sense a symbolic expression of the history and nature of Rome. But the connection of the story of the poem with that history is already in any case explicit: it is presented as the first chapter of it.

A layer of associations of a different kind is furnished by the numerous echoes in the *Aeneid* of situations and phrasing from the *Iliad* and *Odyssey* of Homer, and, to a lesser extent, of others of Virgil's literary predecessors. These only rarely enhance the significance of the Virgilian context in which they appear; and for this reason the reader unacquainted with the Homeric poems will not be at any essential disadvantage, just as a reader of the *Eclogues* need not have read the *Idylls* of Theocritus, and a reader of *Lycidas* need not have read the *Eclogues*. On the other hand, awareness of the extent of the influence of Homeric precedent on the form and content of the *Aeneid* has sometimes led critics in the past to under-estimate wrongly the originality of the Latin poet. The fact is that a comparative study of passages in which the presence of a Homeric 'original' is most obviously felt—say, the Games of Book 5, the Descent to the Underworld of Book 6, the Catalogue of Book 7, or the Duel between the rival heroes at the end of Book 12—is as good a way as any of discovering how Latin, and how personal, the Virgilian passage really is; and the difference of tone and spirit between the old epic and the new is apparent already in the contrast between the intensely personal preoccupations of the heroes of the *Iliad* and *Odyssey* and the public responsibility through which Aeneas' sense of honour (for this motive he shares with Homeric man) finds its expression. It is of course true that in resorting to Homer for the raw material of much of his story Virgil supplies a deficiency in the possibilities of his own imagination; but this deficiency is inherent in his circumstances, not in his powers, and he shows wisdom in resolving it by the means he has chosen. The world of action was outside his direct experience, but the world of Homer he knew well (as it appears in the Homeric poems, that is to say) and his imagination, itself modern, could work with confidence on the material provided by Homeric situations. Moreover the epic as an art form belonged naturally to the legendary past, and Homer provided the only set of terms in which the atmosphere of that past could be re-created. These terms were of course fully *familiar* to the typical educated person in Virgil's day, and accordingly offered to him the same means of rapport with his readers as the familiarity of seventeenth-century readers with the Bible did to Milton. They offered also the simple pleasure of recognition, and the further pleasure (to which the educational habits of the day had sharpened people's susceptibility) of the perception of particular difference in the context of a general similarity. Thus an acquaintance with the Homeric poems, though not essential to the modern reader of Virgil, will bring him nearer to Virgil's mind and to the mind of the readers for whom Virgil wrote; explaining incidentally some details which might otherwise puzzle or offend. In order to know the Homeric poems, for this purpose, it is not necessary to know Greek.

Some of what has been said above will be discussed further in later chapters. It has been touched on now for perspective's sake. We turn now to the story and substance of the poem.

II

THE STORY AND ITS SUBJECT: ROME

THE hero of the *Aeneid* is a legendary Trojan, son of Anchises and the goddess Venus, who fought in and survived the famous Siege of Troy. In Homer's *Iliad* he is twice saved from death in battle by the protecting intervention of a god, a fact which no doubt reflects a tradition that he was favoured by heaven and destined to survive the war. He was famous in the legend for having saved his father and their household gods at the fall of Troy, carrying his father on his shoulders from the burning city. This act of piety became proverbial, so that an author earlier than Virgil, wishing to illustrate the meaning of sarcasm, gives as example 'when we call an unfilial person an Aeneas'.[1] A further development of the legend, current long before Virgil's day, related that Aeneas after his escape from Troy came in due course to Italy, where he settled at Lavinium in Latium, bringing with him the gods which he had preserved. The nature of these gods, which Rome later inherited, was something of a mystery: they were identified by different authorities with various of the gods of classical mythology and also with various holy objects preserved at Rome and near by. But whatever they were—and the mystery about them so far from discrediting their importance increased it—they were believed to symbolize the continuity of the Roman state, in the same way as did the perpetual fire of Vesta, itself associated with these gods that came from Troy and sometimes regarded as one of their number. As well as bringing his gods to Latium Aeneas also became ancestor of a line of kings who ruled there for many generations in the city of Alba Longa, and from this line came the princess who was mother of Romulus, founder of Rome, supposedly by the war-god Mars.

The *Aeneid* tells the story of the migration of the Trojan remnant led by Aeneas from Troy to Italy, their long wanderings on the way and the war which they had to fight in Italy on their arrival. The story embraces many events and seven years of time, including the fall of Troy and the Trojans' final victory in Italy and all that came between. But it is organized in the poem so as to consist of two main phases of action, both belonging to the last year of the story: these are set at Carthage and in Latium respectively, and they are joined by a brief transition (Books 5 and 6) in which the Trojans on their way from Carthage to Latium halt for a short while first in Sicily and then at Cumae on the gulf of Naples. The events of the first six years of the Trojans' experience are not part of the action thus organized, but are narrated as a retrospect by the hero during the phase of the action which is set at Carthage. As the poem stands its outline is as follows.

The Trojans are at sea off the north west of Sicily, bound for the west coast of Italy on what should have been the last leg of their journey, when a sudden storm drives them off their course and brings them, with the loss of one ship, to the African coast near Carthage. They are received with sympathy and kindness by the Carthaginian queen, Dido, to whom Aeneas tells in retrospect the terrible story of the last hours of Troy and the strange and troubled story of his adventures since then. In the course of this—the opening of the story and the hero's narrative of what has gone before—we become aware that the Trojans are bound for Italy by a divine command, progressively revealed to them with the promise of a great future for their posterity, and that they bring with them certain holy symbols of the continuing vitality of defeated Troy. At Carthage the queen falls disastrously in love with Aeneas; an affair develops between them and he begins to fall under her spell. But the thought of his duty prevails over his growing affection; he resolves that he must leave her and journey on; and when he leaves her, she kills herself. Thus ends the first of the two main phases of action in the poem.

Their course and the chances of the weather now bring the Trojans back to the place in Sicily which they had just left at the beginning of the poem when the storm carried them off to Carthage. In Sicily Aeneas holds funeral games in honour of his father. During these resentment flares up among the travel-weary women of the expedition; they set fire to the ships, which are only saved from destruction by a miraculous downpour. Leaving some who have lost heart behind, the Trojans sail on and arrive safely in Italy at Cumae. Here, obeying an injunction given him by his father's ghost in a dream that he had in Sicily, Aeneas with the Sibyl of Cumae for guide goes down into the world of the dead and is shown by his father there a pageant of Roman heroes of the future, symbolic of the purpose of the task laid upon him. The Trojans then sail safely up the coast of Italy to the Tiber mouth. This completes the transition from Carthage to Italy, which acquires a certain unity from the prominence throughout it of the memory of Aeneas' father.

The Trojans now land in Latium and the second main phase of the poem's action, which is also the longest and most elaborate, begins. The newcomers are welcomed by the Latin king, and we learn that oracles have foretold the coming of a stranger from abroad who is to marry the king's daughter and become the ancestor and founder of a great nation. Signs from heaven assure the Trojans also that they have reached the appointed end of their journey, and that this is the land to which fate has willed that they should come. But now they meet with opposition. A neighbouring prince, Turnus, believes himself to have a claim to the hand of the Latin princess, and the queen, her mother, is passionate in support of him. An affray occurs by chance in which some Latins are killed by the Trojans. Feeling runs high; war breaks out; the peoples of Italy from far and wide assemble to help the Latins. Aeneas meanwhile finds allies in some Greek settlers, Arcadians, who have settled on the site where Rome will later stand, and in the neighbouring Etruscans, a powerful people whose king, Mezentius, himself allied with the enemy, has alienated them by his brutalities. In an interval of these activities Aeneas is visited by his goddess mother, who brings him armour made for him by the fire-god at her request: on the shield are prophetic scenes of the future history of Rome. Meanwhile the enemy in the hero's absence attack his camp and come near to capturing it. He returns in time with his reinforcements and the two armies now join battle. Pallas, the son of the Arcadian king, who has led his people to Aeneas' aid, is killed in single combat by the rival leader. Aeneas at this is filled with vengeful fury. Vengeance on the killer eludes him for the present, but he meets the Etruscan tyrant and kills him in single combat. The day's fighting now ends, with the Trojans holding the advantage. A truce follows for the burial of both sides' dead, and during this feeling rises in the Latin town against the war. Taunted by the leader of the peace party, his political rival, the enemy leader declares himself ready to settle matters with Aeneas in a duel. But events move too fast and open warfare is resumed: in the cavalry skirmish which ensues the Latins and their allies again have the worst of it. The offer of a duel between the leaders is renewed, and on the next day a pact is made accordingly. But the pact is broken, Aeneas is wounded, general fighting begins again, and for a while the rival leader carries all before him. But his exaltation subsides in the realization of defeat, and remorse on his

followers' account, when Aeneas, recovered, threatens the Latin city
itself. He goes to face Aeneas, expecting death, and falls wounded
by his spear. Aeneas is about to spare him, when he sees that he
wears a sword-belt taken as a trophy from the body of the Arcadian
prince: in a burst of rage he thrusts his sword through the other's
heart. Thus ends the second main phase of the poem's action, and
with it the poem itself.

Woven into the telling of this story and affecting decisively the
course of it are the activities of supernatural powers, on the one hand
an impersonal Destiny which wills the coming of the Trojans to
Italy as an event necessary to the future birth of the Roman people
and the rise of Rome to greatness in the world, and on the other
hand a number of individual powers endowed with separate personalities and separate wills. These latter are represented in human
shapes and with human mentalities, in the terms of an anthro-
pomorphizing mythology which Greek and Roman literature, and
to some extent society, had inherited from Homer. Literal belief in
this mythology was of course obsolete generally among the educated
in Virgil's day. But belief was still widely prevalent in the reality of
divine powers with private wills, eternally active in the world and
intervening decisively in the affairs of men and nations. In the
Aeneid, as its prologue announces, a principal cause of all that
happens is the personal opposition of the goddess Juno to the purpose
of Destiny, an opposition due to her hatred of Troy and her fear of
the promised greatness of Rome as threatening the hopes which she
cherishes for her own favourite, Carthage. It is the will of Juno,
acting through the agency of lesser powers, which causes the storm
at the beginning of the poem and the outbreak of war in Italy at the
beginning of its second half, thus setting in motion the two main
phases of action which terminate, ironically, in the deaths of Juno's
human favourites Dido and Turnus, the Carthaginian queen and the
Italian prince. Similarly it is the will of Juno which provokes the
mutiny of the Trojan women in Sicily, in a last attempt to prevent
the arrival in Italy taking place, and the attack on the camp in
Aeneas' absence which is the first engagement of the war. Venus on
the other hand because of her personal interest in Aeneas assists the
design of Destiny, and enlists the help of other Olympians on her
son's behalf—of Neptune to ensure the Trojans a safe passage from
Sicily to Italy on the last stage of their journey, and of Vulcan to
make the armour for Aeneas which he wears in the final battles.
These examples are in illustration, not an exhaustive list, of the

activities of the two goddesses in the poem. By contrast Jupiter, to whose power that of the other gods is subject, is concerned to super-intend the fulfilment of the purpose of Destiny, with which his own will is identified. His attention is intermittent and he may tem-porarily and within limits indulge the opposed purpose of a sub-ordinate power such as Juno, but he will not allow the grand design of providence to be frustrated, and he intervenes to protect it at every crucial turn of events—when for instance Aeneas as Carthage is in danger of forgetting his mission, or when the Trojan ships are in danger in Sicily, or when the Trojan camp seems to be on the point of being captured or the Trojan army about to fall into an ambush. The relations between the goddesses and Jupiter are exhibited in dramatic form in conversation scenes in heaven. These scenes are also convenient to the poet's purpose in enabling him to introduce prophecies of the future into the narrative. Other scenes of the supernatural serve to provide pictorial decoration or to create atmosphere: for instance Neptune as he skims the waves in his chariot with nymphs and lesser sea-gods gambolling about him, and Vulcan at work in his forge with his Cyclops-artisans, or on the other hand the fiends and monsters, Rumour full of tongues and eyes and ears, the Fury Allecto, the fire-breathing giant Cacus, the Dira which is sent to seal the fate of the doomed warrior in the final scene of all.[2] The theological apparatus in the *Aeneid* to some extent serves purposes which are purely literary. But it also reflects real feelings about the working in the world of a law of destiny and of independent supernatural wills.

From the brief accounts given above of the story of the poem and the representation of the gods in it the close affinity of the *Aeneid* to the Homeric poems will already be apparent. It combines the sub-jects of both wanderings and war. From the *Odyssey* it adopts the structural device whereby an important part of the story is narrated in a retrospect by the principal character. From the *Iliad* it adopts the themes of the camp endangered while the hero is absent from the field and of the hero's friend killed in combat by his rival and the hero's quest for vengeance on the killer. It echoes many striking individual episodes:[3] the storm, the games, the descent into the underworld, the catalogue of allies, the making of a marvellous shield for the hero by the fire-god, the night adventure, the duel to the death between the rival heroes, and much more which need not be entered into now. It depicts the gods in council, Juno's animosity against Troy, a mother goddess' solicitude for her human son, and so on. As well as absorbing these and many other motifs from the Homeric poems, the *Aeneid* is set in the same legendary age with them. It is in a manner a sequel to the *Iliad*, and its action is contemporary with that of the *Odyssey*. The Trojans, in the third book, come like Ulysses to the land of the Cyclops and find there a surviving castaway of Ulysses' crew. Ulysses himself is still marooned on Calypso's island, and will be there for some years yet, when the Trojans reach their destination in Italy. We meet or hear in the *Aeneid* of other familiar figures beside the hero from the Homeric tale of Troy, the Trojan Helenus in Epirus, the Greek Diomede at Arpi in Italy.[4] But while the *Aeneid* is thus a reflection of the Homeric poems and set in time in the Homeric world, it is set in place largely in pre-Roman Italy and looks forward persistently to the world of Rome. The prologue to the poem declares that the story is of 'a man who came . . . to Italy, to Lavinium, afflicted much by trials on land and sea through the power of the gods above, and tried by war too, that he might found a city, and bring his gods to Latium, beginning of the Latin race and the Alban kings and the high city of Rome herself'. This affirmation of the continuity of the *Aeneid's* story with the history of Rome is repeated in more detail and with greater emphasis in the prophetic speech of Jupiter to Venus which follows shortly after the action of the poem opens: Aeneas will reign at Lavinium, his son Ascanius will found Alba Longa and Aeneas' descendants will reign there for three hundred years, and then a princess of the royal line will bear a son to Mars, Romulus the founder of Rome. In two later prophetic passages in the centre of the poem, the pageant of future heroes seen in the underworld and the pageant of scenes from history depicted on Aeneas' shield, the history of Rome itself is in turn carried from the foundation of the city to the poet's own day. The *Aeneid* is thus presented as the first chapter of a story which is still continuing. This is one reason why it seems to end abruptly, with much still untold, and to have structurally the character of an episode, a grand and internally complex episode, rather than of a completed story.

When the story told in the *Aeneid* ends, the foundation of Rome for which it prepares the way is still three hundred years ahead in the future. But the presence and personality of Rome is felt strongly in the poem throughout, and especially in the central part of it as the Trojans approach and reach and recognize their promised land and the journey of the hero himself is prolonged to the very place where Rome itself will one day be. If one thinks of the terms in which the personality of one's own country comes to mind, one will recognize among them most or all of those in which Virgil has communicated in the *Aeneid* the personality of Rome. The great events, and especially the great crises, of its history are evoked in the series of scenes depicted on the shield which Vulcan made and Venus brings to Aeneas when the day of battle approaches. The great men who established the Roman state in its early years, and those who later guided it through its gravest trials are displayed to Aeneas in the underworld in the vision of the souls awaiting the time of their incarnation. The Romans are called 'the people of the Roman gown' in allusion to their distinctive national dress, and the characteristic institutions of the Roman state are exhibited in the story as brought or invented by the Trojan immigrants or as existing already among the native peoples who were to be joint ancestors of the Romans with them. Thus the Roman custom of cloaking the head in the act of sacrifice is enjoined on Aeneas by the seer Helenus before his arrival in Italy; the exhibition of drill on horseback known to the Romans as the *lusus Troiae* is given by the young Trojans in the Aeneid at Anchises' funeral games; the institution of the prophetic Sibylline Books, consulted by the Romans in times of national crisis, is promised by Aeneas in his prayer in Apollo's temple at Cumae before his descent into the world of the dead; the Roman practice of opening for war and closing in peace the double gates of the arch of Janus is presented as a custom already existing in Latium when the Trojans come; the worship of Hercules at the Great Altar in the cattle-market, observed in the Rome of the poet's day, is witnessed by Aeneas in Evander's Pallanteum; the procedure of a Roman state funeral is reflected in the ceremony with which the fallen Arcadian prince is escorted to his home.[5]

It will be noticed too that the landscape becomes more visible as the Trojans near their destination. They land in Italy at Cumae on the gulf of Naples, in a region where Virgil spent much of his life, and one charged with moving associations because of the naval war of 38–6 B.C. between Octavian's forces and those of Pompey's son Sextus, in which it was a base of operations. The background of the action here is provided by the cave-temple of Apollo, the promontory of Misenum and the wooded hillsides ringing lake Avernus. The Trojans proceed from Cumae up the coast, and after a moonlight voyage made brilliantly visible by the poet they reach the estuary of the Tiber, described in another brilliantly visible scene: the associations of the approach by sea for the returning traveller are exploited here, as in the earlier description of the first landfall made by the Trojans in south-east Italy,[6] an experience surely familiar to those in the poet's day who came home that way from travel or service in the east. As the envoys sent to King Latinus approach the Latin capital they first come to a park outside the town in which the young men of the community are engaged in sports and exercises, anticipating the Campus Martius of historical Rome. The king himself receives them in a vast pillared building which is both temple and council chamber, scene also of ritual banquets, set high on a hill, with statues of former kings before the doors; a description of which every detail is applicable to the great temple of Jupiter on the Capitol at Rome, an architectural feature as significant of Rome as St. Paul's or the parliament building is of London.[7] Next, the assembling of the Italian peoples gives occasion for a panoramic review of Italian landscapes: mountains and lakes and isolated temples, streams coursing down hillsides or across plainland or through valleys to the sea, shallow rivers with rush-grown beds, high peaks and craggy rocks and hills topped with fortress walls. Meanwhile Aeneas and his men row up the Tiber as it winds along between wooded banks, their shields reflected in the water among the over-hanging boughs of trees, until under the noonday sun they come to the village which stands on the site of future Rome, a handful of dwellings and a grove near by in which stands the Great Altar of Hercules, a familiar landmark in the poet's Rome; later his host conducts Aeneas through his village kingdom showing him other familiar landmarks as they go. Glimpses of local fable add local colour and deepen the sense of legendary antiquity: the fire-breathing giant Cacus, and Picus who was the witch Circe's husband and turned by her into a bird, and Cycnus changed by grief into a swan, and Umbro the snake-charming magician, and Caeculus begotten by the fire-god himself in the ashes of the hearth.[8]

Thus Virgil in the course of his poem expresses the idea of Rome and Italy, which to him are mutually complementary concepts, in terms of history, people, customs, legend and scenery; and through the medium of prophecy he keeps the reader throughout aware that the story he tells of events in the Homeric age is only the beginning of the much longer story of which the birth and rise and achievement of Rome are later chapters. He is of course strongly aware and proud of the aspect of Rome's greatness which is power: Rome, *rerum pulcherrima* in his *Georgics*, is here *alta, maxima, maxima rerum, potens, incluta*, and the Romans are *rerum domini*, 'lords of the world', granted by the gods an empire without end in time, *imperium sine fine*, and bringing law and order to the peoples that they govern. The substance of this is a matter of history, but there is of course sometimes an element of rhetorical hyperbole in the terms which Virgil uses: thus, the expression *orbis* ('world'), used of the extent of the Roman empire, does not in a writer of this time imply anything larger than the vast extent it had already attained—Cicero could say of Pompey a generation before that he had made the bounds of the empire coextensive with the limits of the 'world'; Brutus could speak of himself and his fellow-tyrannicides as 'liberators of the world'; Ovid could claim that Jupiter surveying 'the whole world' from his eminence on the Capitol could see no land that was not under the rule of Rome.[9] The point is worth remarking because a legitimate pride in the greatness of a man's country has often been associated with other attitudes that Virgil does not share. He nowhere says for instance that Rome's destiny authorizes unlimited conquest; or that Rome's wars have been prompted by benevolence, to bring the advantages of good government to others; or that destiny has chosen the Romans in acknowledgement of their merits or as agents of a moral purpose for the betterment of all mankind. There is in Virgil no idea corresponding to that of Manifest Destiny or of the White Man's Burden or to the supposition that 'God has called us to civilize the world'.[10] The greatness of Rome, and the prevalence of law and order in the Roman empire, are facts to him, as they are to history; and he further affirms that Rome's greatness has been willed by fate from the beginning. But he does not moralize the process as a 'mission' to improve mankind.[11] Nor, as becomes very clear in the telling of his story, is he unaware of the cost to others, as well as to Romans, that the rise of Rome to greatness has involved.

The *Aeneid* is in a real sense the poet's tribute to his country. For the idea was abroad at the time that the man of letters can serve his country as well as the soldier and statesman. He serves it, as Virgil's younger contemporary Propertius hoped to do in his Roman elegies, and as Livy conceived himself as doing in his monumental Roman history, by writing worthily about it.[12] And he serves it by enriching its culture, as Cicero was told by Caesar he had done through his achievement in oratory, and as he set out to do in the long series of his philosophical writings, extending the capacities of the Latin language and creating a new department of Latin literature.[13] The most exalted department of literature according to ancient ideas was the epic, and the greatest work of literature was the epic of Homer. The *Aeneid* was thus intended to be the Latin counterpart of the *Iliad* and *Odyssey* and worthy to stand comparison with them. But though a contemporary boasted, while Virgil was at work on his poem, that 'something greater than the Iliad is in the making',[14] the *Aeneid* is not conceived in a spirit of rivalry, to outdo the Homeric epics: the obligation to them which it openly exhibits is too far-reaching. Rather, it expresses the harmonization of the Greek and Roman elements in the culture of Virgil's world. This reconciliation of the old antagonism, as well as the antagonism itself, is foreseen in the story of the poem too, where a Greek people opens the way of success to the Trojans, a Greek hero dies to win them a home in Italy, and Aeneas at his parting from Helenus in Epirus looks forward to a day when the two peoples will be one in mind and spirit: 'let that not fail to be the care of our children's children'.[15]

III

THE HERO: AENEAS

In the famous scene in the world of the dead which comes in the middle of the *Aeneid* the hero is shown a succession of the leaders who in a still distant future will shape the history of the Roman state. Such pageants were familiar in Roman life in less extraordinary contexts. The statues of the great generals and statesmen of the past stood arrayed in order on the Capitol and in the Forum. Figures of those who had honoured their families by high achievement in the service of the state were carried in procession at the funerals of members of the families which they had adorned. The famous names of the past were ready on the lips of an orator or moralist to illustrate the virtues that they embodied: 'Let us then follow the example of our Roman forebears, men such as Brutus, Camillus, Ahala, the Decii, Curius, Fabricius, Maximus, the Scipios, Lentulus, Aemilius, and countless others who laid the foundations on which this commonwealth now stands.'[1] Virgil's Aeneas is of course conceived as the first of this long succession and in a sense representative of them, and his endeavours as an epitome of all the effort and sacrifice which had gone to the making of the Rome that Virgil knew: 'so heavy a task it was to found the Roman race'. In the prologue of the poem the hero appears as 'a man harassed by many trials on land and sea and suffering in war also, that he might found a city . . . whence should come the Latin race and the Alban kings and the high city of Rome itself'; and when we first are shown him in the story he bears with him the gods of Troy that are symbols of the continuity of Troy and Rome, as later he will bear on his shoulder the prophetic shield which through the scenes depicted on it is symbol of the 'fame and fortune' of the Roman people.

It is distinctive of the role of Aeneas in the *Aeneid* as 'first begetter of the Roman race'[2] that he is conceived as the instrument of a providential purpose. Fate has willed that he should do and suffer what he does to begin the process in history that leads to the birth and rise of Rome. It is 'by fate's will' that he becomes an exile from his homeland. 'Fate holds out the promise' to him and his men of a new dwelling-place where they can settle in peace and Troy can rise again under the favour of heaven. He has sailed from Troy 'follow-ing the will of fate declared to us'. And fate does not only promise, it commands: 'the command of heaven drove' Aeneas from Carthage: 'the fateful purpose of the gods commanded' the Trojans to seek a home in Italy: Aeneas and his men are 'summoned on and ever onward by the call of fate'.[3] But because another power, itself divine, resents and opposes the purpose of providence the hero and his men, and others too, must pay a heavy price in toil and suffering in order that the mission laid upon them may be fulfilled, and this is the story of the *Aeneid*: 'so heavy a task it was to found the Roman race', as the poet says at the beginning of his story, and 'so much have I endured to win this land', as the hero says at the end.[4] He is 'harassed by trials on land and sea', 'harassed by fearful dangers', 'tried by affliction through the fate of Troy'.[5] And the purpose is to found a city, 'an abiding city' as he prays, through which a great future is promised to his children's children.[6] The Trojans are com-manded at first to leave their home in total ignorance of their destination, 'not knowing whither fate is carrying us, where it is given us to end our journey', and the revelation is made by degrees: first in a riddling oracle which they do not understand, then in a vision which names the promised land, then by a seer who sets them on their way, and lastly in pictorial but still mysterious revelations which give a glimpse of the future of their descendants many cen-turies ahead.[7]

In much of this there is a strange analogy with the story of Abraham as told in the book of Genesis and recalled in the epistle to the Hebrews: 'Now the Lord said unto Abraham, Get thee out from thy country, and from thy kindred, and from thy father's house, unto a land that I will show thee: And I will make of thee a great nation, and I will bless thee, and make thy name great. . . . So Abraham departed, as the Lord had spoken unto him'; and again, 'By faith Abraham, when he was called to go out into a place which he should after receive for an inheritance, obeyed and went out, not knowing whither he went . . . for he looked for a city which hath foundations, whose builder and maker is God.'[8] Like Abraham Aeneas receives a command from heaven; is told to leave his own homeland for a destination still unrevealed; has the promise of a great future for his posterity; has the hope of 'an abiding city'. The analogy has naturally coloured the story of Aeneas with a symbolic significance for later readers which the poet of the Aeneid could not have foreseen. It also invites attention to the fact that the type represented by Virgil's Aeneas is without apparent precedent in Greek and Latin literature. There is no sign that the conception of Aeneas as a man with a mission or vocation owes anything to the memory of the ethical mission of Socrates, who was indeed, as he believed, 'commanded by the god in oracles and dreams and in every way in which ever a man was commanded' to labour to persuade the Athenians to care for moral goodness.[9] The figure of the Hercules of legend, afflicted by the enmity of Juno and oppressed by long and arduous labours, is no doubt reflected in some aspects of the person of Aeneas.[10] But there is nothing in the story of Hercules (though he came to be thought of as a benefactor of the human race) of service to a providential purpose. The conception embodied in Aeneas of a man called to serve a high purpose in history at the behest of heaven is Virgil's own, as far as can be judged.

Because Aeneas is depicted as guided by a command from above, and counselled and reminded from above through oracles and dreams and other kinds of revelation, he is sometimes felt by readers to be no more than a puppet or automaton, controlled mechanically by forces outside himself, and without character of his own. This is apt to be felt especially by one who comes to the *Aeneid* from the Homeric poems, in which the scope of the rich individuality of the characters is not much or often limited by concern for public responsibilities. But in fact, though Aeneas is commanded by a higher power, he is not compelled, and it is precisely the circumstance that his will is free and his decisions his own that distinguishes his situation from that of other characters in the story whose wills have ceased to be their own because external powers have taken control of them.[11] Aeneas could have disregarded the bidding to leave his own country and sail into the unknown; his own wish, as he tells Dido, was to stay in the homeland that he knew. He could have stayed at Carthage with Dido and shared the city that she had founded. He could have settled in Sicily, as he was later briefly tempted to do, 'forgetting' as the poet says 'the call of fate'.[12] The story makes it plain that it was only by a sustained effort of will that he was able to confront and surmount the successive trials that his *fortuna*—his doom to suffer in the conflict between the design of providence and Juno's resistance to it—imposed on him: 'sick at heart with overwhelming care', 'tossed on the surge of troubled thoughts', 'turning his anxious thoughts this way and that', 'forbidden sleep by care', 'his heart heavy as he pondered all the dangers'.[13] The impression that the poet gives of him is of a man wrestling with extreme fatigue. The land to which the Trojans must journey is 'never nearer', 'always elusive'. Aeneas sighs with envy at the sight of others—the Tyrians at Carthage, the Trojans in Epirus— who have reached their journey's end: 'fortunate these, whose new city's walls are already rising', 'fortunate you whose trials are over, who have found rest, who are not called to plough the sea in quest of this Italy, that is never nearer, while we are beckoned endlessly on by fate'.[14]

Again, because of the control which Aeneas exercises in this way over his feelings it is sometimes objected that he lacks warmth of feeling, is exempt from ordinary human emotions. But this notion too is contradicted by the evidence of the story, in which Aeneas' sensibility appears at every parting and every loss, and in which we meet him first in a moment of terror and leave him at the end in an outburst of anger.[15] In the last hours of Troy he is possessed with the blind rage of despair.[16] In the decision to leave Carthage he feels emotions so strong that he must 'wrestle' to control them: emotions that 'shake his soul', and 'fill all his being'.[17] The death of his friend Pallas provokes him to a revengeful fury that makes seem perverse any conception of him as a passionless man,[18] and is at the same time strangely in contrast with his usually compassionate nature.

For it is clear that compassion is a principal element in Virgil's image of his hero. It shows itself in every context except that of Pallas' death, and not only in Aeneas' relations with those near him but in his dealings with strangers, subordinates and even enemies: with the faint hearts who forsake his cause in Sicily, with the un- known sufferers in the world of the dead, with the young soldier whom he kills in battle defending his wounded father, with the nameless dead of his own party to whom his first thoughts go in the moment of victory, even (on a different level of experience) with an unlucky competitor in the games that he holds in his dead father's honour.[19] This quality in the hero is reflected, with others, in the epithet *pius* which is recurrently applied to him; for *pietas* includes pity as well as piety, as the derivation of these words from it shows. In the first context in the poem in which Aeneas is called *pius* he is grieving for comrades whom he believes to be lost; in the next he is thinking of his responsibilities to the men whom he leads; in the next he is forcing himself to make duty prevail over sympathy after his parting scene with Dido;[20] and the context in which the word is applied to him more often than in any other, that of paying burial honours to friends, is one in which religious duty is joined with human feeling.[21]

To apply the epithet *pius* to Aeneas is not Virgil's invention, but an echo of proverbial usage, in which it alluded to the hero's legendary act of religious and filial 'piety' in saving his household gods and his father from burning Troy. It is this which is recalled when Aeneas announces himself to a (supposed) stranger with the words 'I am *pius* Aeneas . . . carrying with me my gods from Troy across the seas . . .'[22] He is in that passage not so much claiming a moral quality as identifying himself by the achievement for which he was known in legend. The traditional religious piety of Aeneas is further illustrated in the *Aeneid* by his frequent and careful acts of ritual observance (a Roman characteristic),[23] and of course (though the poet does not so use the words *pius* and *pietas* in the story as to mark this connection) by his obedience to the command from above which is his mission: it is thus a major theme. Another major theme is the *pietas* of Aeneas towards his father, 'comfort in all my cares and trials', whose funeral honours are the subject of the fifth book of the poem and for love of whom (*pietas*) Aeneas braves in the sixth book the terrors of the world below.[24] After saving his father from the fall of Troy he shares with him, until the old man's death, the leadership of the Trojans in their long journeying, and in the course of this it becomes clear that Anchises is a source of encouragement and inspiration to his son in the execution of his mission. It is at his insistence that the decision is made to obey the oracles and make the break with their old home. It is he who hastens their departure after the pleasant interlude in Epirus. It is his ghost which troubles Aeneas' conscience in dreams as he dallies at Carthage. It is his ghost again which strengthens Aeneas' resolve when it wavers in Sicily after the mutiny of the women and firing of the ships. It is he who shows Aeneas in the underworld the vision of his Roman posterity which is to make him rejoice in the promised land he finds in Italy and 'fire his heart with the hope of future glory'. When Aeneas in Latium knows by a sign that he has reached his journey's end his first thought after giving thanks to heaven is of his father.[25]

The story of Aeneas' experience is narrated in three phases, which might be described briefly as quest, arrival, victory. The first phase extends through Books 1.1–5.699, the second through 5.700–8.731, and the third (Aeneas being absent from the scene in the ninth book) through Books 10–12. In this development of events there is a corresponding change not indeed of the hero's character—there is no probable indication of that—but of his situation and consequently of his attitude.

The first phase begins, in time though not in the narrative order of the poem, with the awful memory of the fall of Troy. In telling the story to Dido Aeneas vows in the name of his homeland and his fallen friends that on that fatal night he exposed himself to every possible hazard and deserved (i.e. as being what he desired) to die in the fighting.[26] This plainly is what Roman sentiment would approve, and when Aeneas speaks of himself also as acting 'more from blind impulse than from reasoned hope'[27] in the furious resistance which he makes for as long as resistance is possible he is not confessing a failure of self-control but describing a reaction that to a Roman would seem proper and natural in a man whose country was falling in ruins about him. If he escapes and survives it is for his family's sake, and with the sanction of three prompting visions—the apparitions of Hector and Venus and Creusa.[28] These visions sanction his escape and foreshadow his mission to found a new Troy; but the mission does not become positive until he is established as leader of the Trojan remnant in the hinterland and receives the bidding of the oracles to leave his homeland and set out for a destination that is at first unrevealed. The progressive clarification of this instruction is, as has been earlier observed, a theme in the story of the Wanderings which follows. Another theme in that story, also already remarked on, is the active participation of Aeneas' father in the leadership of the expedition until his death in Sicily just before the formal action of the poem begins. This does not necessarily imply any infirmity in Aeneas' own purpose: it reflects the Roman feeling for the position of the father in the family and the poet's conception of the special affection prevailing between this father and this son. The principal theme of the story of the Wanderings (and it is not altogether adequately sustained) is long and weary journeying through fearsome trials—horrors, plague, storm, encounters with monsters, deluded hopes—in obedience to the divine command. These past experiences and the mood engendered by them are evoked in the opening scenes of the poem: Aeneas encourages his men after the storm with the thought of the worse trials that they have survived: he sees depicted on the doors of the temple at Carthage scenes reminiscent of the Trojan war; he complains (to a stranger in whom he recognizes a goddess) that his obedience to the gods is rewarded with affliction.[29] It is in this mood that he is exposed to the temptations of Carthage, and it is legitimate to imagine (though whether this is the poet's intention we cannot tell) that fatigue and discouragement and the loss of the father who shared his troubles with him have left him vulnerable at this point. In the episode which follows he is in danger of forgetting his mission, and he is represented (how plausibly the reader of the *Aeneid* must judge for himself) as in danger again of forgetting it in Sicily after the mutiny of the women and firing of the ships. Warned by a god at Carthage and encouraged by a dream of his father in Sicily, but in both cases by the exercise of his own will, he persists with his task.

The second phase of Aeneas' story now begins, with the arrival of the Trojans in Italy. At Cumae he is promised by the Sibyl that the hazards of the long voyage are safely past.[30] In Latium the fulfilment of a prophecy, confirmed, in answer to a prayer, by a sign from heaven, gives him the assurance that he is here finally at his journey's end and that this is the new homeland promised to him by the fates.[31] This assurance is presently confirmed further by the fulfilment of another prophecy and the explicit statement of the Tiber-god, appearing to him in a vision.[32] Ever since the Trojans left their old home in the Troad they have been in search of a new home appointed for them by the gods: the word *patria* (homeland) is recurrent in the poem: 'I seek a home that is to be mine in Italy', 'there (in Italy) is my heart, my home', 'these brave spirits who have won this home for us with their lives'.[33] The hero has now at last found his new home; and there, as it proves, he is welcomed as a man of destiny whose coming has been foretold in oracles to the people of the land. To the Latin king he is 'the man whom fate calls' to be parent by the king's daughter of a famous posterity; to the king of the Arcadians who live on the site of future Rome he is 'the man whom the gods call' to lead the native Etruscans in war against their tyrant ex-king and his allies; to the Tiber-god he is one 'long awaited by the Latin land'.[34] The Tiber-god assures him also that the gods once angry are against him no more, and that he need feel no fear of the war that is impending. His mother Venus gives him the same assurance, and a sign from heaven, and divine armour made for him by the fire-god. He is joined by powerful allies from Italy itself, and goes to confront his enemies as 'leader of Italy and Troy together'.[35] Not least, he has seen in the underworld at Cumae a revelation of the future greatness of his descendants, the cause for which fate has required him to endure all that he has endured so far.

Thus when Aeneas arrives at the beginning of the tenth book to do battle with the forces which oppose the Trojans he is now, in the

third phase of the story, in a very different situation from that of the
tired and troubled wanderer of its first phase. The weary journeying
is over. The promised land, sought for seven years, is attained. The
vision of the future is revealed. The favour of the gods is assured.
Aeneas stands as defender of his homeland, leader of a powerful
alliance, wearer of divine armour; and the context, now a military
one, is congenial to his talents as a Homeric and as a Roman hero,
however uncongenial to his humaner inclinations. It is not surprising
that he is completely confident: confident already in the previous
phase, when his mother's sign warned him that war was approaching, confident now as he arrives at the scene of action, confident at
the prospect of combat with the Etruscan tyrant, confident at the
prospect of combat with his rival Turnus, assuring his men that
Jupiter and fate are on their side.[36] Meanwhile the reader has
learned that the enemy have the ruling powers of heaven against
them, engaged as they are in 'an unholy war, defying the warnings
of the gods and thwarting their will', and that even Juno hopes at
most to delay the victory of the Trojans which she no longer aspires
to avert.[37] The story in this part of the poem is of the achievement
by Aeneas of a victory already assured, and his role forfeits some
interest on that account. It is noticeable that he is represented as
almost ostentatiously selfless: he has no personal motive, he seeks to
settle in Italy only because the gods have appointed him a place
there, if victorious he will leave the royal rights of Latinus unim-
paired, he asks only some land on which to build his city and the
hand of the princess already offered to him.[38] This last motif, the
hand of the princess, belongs to the original legend of Aeneas'
coming to Italy, and it is necessary to the conception of Aeneas'
victory as leading to the foundation of a royal race in which the
qualities of Trojan and Italian are united. It is also cause of the
rival leader Turnus' hostility to Aeneas. But as a motive of Aeneas
in his hostility to Turnus it is suppressed in favour of a motive
adopted from Homer's *Iliad*, the anger of the hero against the man
who killed his friend, the young Arcadian Pallas. This anger extends
to all the enemy in the first heat of it, when Aeneas first learns of
Pallas' death, and it expresses itself, at that time, in brutalities
which are altogether at variance with the hero's usual humanity,
and indeed with the standards of the poet's civilized contemporaries.
He taunts a victim with the thought that he will lie unburied. He
takes prisoners to be sacrificed alive, in cold blood, at Pallas'
funeral.[39] There is Homeric precedent for this of course, and the

Roman world was not a gentle one; but human sacrifice was
barbaric to authors such as Cicero and Livy, and Virgil's presentation of Aeneas here remains extraordinary.[40] On the other hand the
killing of Turnus by Aeneas at the end of the story is on a different
plane; for this is on the battlefield, and the duty to avenge a friend
was strongly felt. Turnus had killed Pallas, and himself accepts the
victor's right to kill him in his turn (12.931). Aeneas' act in doing
so is made by the poet to result from a momentary flaring up of
anger, stirred by the memory of his friend's death, in a normally
compassionate nature. It would seem to Virgil's readers poetically
just.

   It remains to say something about the state of Aeneas' feelings in
his relationship with Dido. To some readers he has seemed a stiff
and unfeeling figure in this; to others a romantic lover making an
agonizing sacrifice of his personal happiness to his duty. The poet
has in fact told the story with the emphasis almost wholly on the
experience of Dido, and has been far from explicit about the role of
Aeneas. Moreover the indications which he has given seem at times
to be in contradiction one with another—though some may feel that
this contradiction is not irreconcilable with the facts of human
nature. After the scene in which Aeneas is exposed to Dido's
entreaties and reproaches, when she has learned of his intention to
go on his way, he is said to be 'shattered by the power of love'. But
when he received the warning from heaven that prompted his
departure his immediate reaction was one of 'eagerness' to obey.[41]
And when he later encounters Dido's ghost in the world of the dead
his speech is full of affection and sympathy for her but contains
nothing to suggest the feelings of one who has himself suffered a
devastating loss.

   Because the poet says so little about Aeneas in telling this part of
the story it is not possible to do more than guess at his conception of
Aeneas' feelings. But it may help if we recall how different were the
connotations of *amor*, as a passion, for him and his contemporaries
from those which our own literature associates with romantic love.
To the love poets of Virgil's day love in this sense is a compulsive
power which makes a man utterly absorbed in a woman to the
exclusion of all the normal values of society around him. To Cicero
writing as a moralist *amor* renders its victim shameless and irresponsible.[42] In recent memory Antony, ruler of half the Roman
world, had fallen under the spell of Cleopatra and given himself up
to wanton enjoyments with her, forgetting his dignity and his

responsibilities, and, worse still, subordinating Roman interests to
the ambitions of a foreign queen.[43] It seems very likely that the
strong impression made by this has actually coloured Virgil's story
of the doings of Dido and Aeneas: they too are said to be 'heedless
of honour and dignity', and rumour has it that they have become
'slaves of a shameful infatuation, sunk in wanton pleasuring together
all the winter long':[44] and when the messenger of the gods comes to
warn Aeneas of his danger he finds him wearing a jewelled sword
and a cloak of golden and purple stuff, not unlike Antony as
described by a later writer 'with a golden sceptre, and a scimitar
at his side, and a purple robe fastened with jewels'.[45] This is not to
say that we are to think of the two relationships as exactly or even
closely similar. But it will be seen how the compulsive element in
love was readily conceived as a morally dangerous addiction, which
a man might in a rational moment be 'eager' to escape but be able
to escape only at the cost of a painful and even agonizing effort.
Further, this compulsive element in a man's feeling for a woman
can co-exist with other strong feelings from which it is conceived as
distinct—with hate, as testified by Catullus in a famous couplet,[46]
on the one hand, or on the other hand with a warm but rational
affection. Such affection Aeneas feels for Dido from the beginning
to the end of the story, and it is reflected in terms such as *optima Dido*
('his dear Dido': the epithet here is the one commonly applied to a
loved parent) and *dulci amore* ('with tenderness', which the poet
uses of the tone with which Aeneas addresses Dido's ghost in the
underworld, after her tragic end). The pain that Aeneas feels for
Dido in their parting is that of affectionate sympathy. The pain
that he feels for himself is nearer to the pain of a necessary surgical
operation than to the pain of sacrificing something supremely
valuable.

IV

THE SECONDARY HEROES: DIDO AND TURNUS

IF Aeneas' mission brings suffering to him, it brings both suffering and disaster to others whose lives it crosses, and for the same cause—the conflict between the wills of higher powers over the destiny of Rome. Dido for love of Aeneas and Turnus in enmity become victims, tragic victims, of this conflict. There is much that corresponds in the stories of the two as Virgil tells them: the heroic quality of their persons, their ultimate innocence, and above all the sympathy with which the poet enters into their experience. This awareness of the obverse of his story runs as a counter-theme through all the *Aeneid*. For what happens to Dido and to Turnus is an example of the price paid in history by the other side. It is now time to consider the two stories in turn.

Before Dido appears we have learned something of her past: how she escaped from Tyre after the murder of the king her husband and came with a band of followers to found a new city at Carthage. When she appears it is in the role of queen, active, admired, beautiful and attended with all the honours of her royal condition. She receives the Trojans with generous sympathy. But almost at once she begins to be overcome by an obsessive love for Aeneas—inflicted on her, as the story is told, by the irresistible will of a higher power. She tries at first to resist this because she has vowed her affections to the memory of her dead husband and because to be the slave of desire offends her self-respect and sense of dignity. But her sister with good intentions encourages her to yield to her feelings and to hope for marriage with Aeneas. His stay is prolonged by the winter season and the refitting of his ships. By a fatal combination of circumstances (contrived, again, by a higher power) Dido and he are brought together alone during a hunting expedition: Aeneas becomes her lover, and from now on lives openly with her as such. Enjoying their love they are felt by those about them to neglect their dignity. Dido is wholly absorbed in Aeneas: he under the influence of her personality and her strong affection begins to forget the duty laid on him to found the new Troy in Italy: he begins to behave as Dido's consort.[1] Dido for her part thinks of their liaison as a marriage, though nothing to this effect has passed between them. She knows of course that Aeneas believes himself called to Italy, but she has no cause herself to think the call compelling.[2] Aeneas however becomes uneasy, and presently the conviction comes to him (through an abrupt and insistent warning from above) that he must part from Dido before he is involved beyond retreat.[3] He makes plans for departure, but knowing the intensity of Dido's feeling he delays to tell her, waiting for an occasion to break the news of his decision gently. As a result she hears of his plans before he can tell her and supposes that he has meant to leave without her knowledge. A dreadful scene follows in which Aeneas, himself in great distress and controlling himself with difficulty, can do no more than acknowledge his debt to her and remind her that he is not a free agent: he is compelled by the gods' command and his responsibility to his son to go on to Italy: he begs her not to make the parting harder for him as well as her. Of his feeling for her or the reason for the secrecy of his preparations he has nothing to say. Dido's reply to this is a speech of blazing anger, at the end of which she leaves him standing, shaken and afraid. He suppresses his own feelings, for both of them, and goes about the business of preparing his departure. Dido's anger is followed by reaction: she cannot yet endure to be without him and sends her sister to beg him at least to delay his going. Aeneas, agonized, is still unyielding. He never sees or speaks to Dido again in this world.

At this point Dido begins to dwell on the thought of death.[4] She imagines that she hears her former husband calling her. She experiences in dreams a sense of awful desolation. The idea forms itself in her mind of killing herself on a pyre prepared for her own burning, together with such reminders of Aeneas as remain in the palace, garments and arms and the bed which they had shared together. Concealing her real purpose she pretends that these preparations are required for a magic ceremony which will cure her love or bring Aeneas back to her. The pyre is built. And now it is night, and Dido lies awake, tormented by conflicting emotions, love and anger and remorse. All her thoughts come back to the conviction that death (deserved, she feels)[5] is the only way out of the misery of her frustrated love and the shame of what she has abandoned for it. Meanwhile Aeneas is sleeping aboard his ship, ready now to sail. He wakes from a dream with the conviction that he must sail at once, lest he be prevented. He starts up and gives the order to cast off. When morning comes Dido sees the ships out at sea. She thinks for a moment of armed pursuit; but it is too late; in a passion of revengeful fury she invokes a curse on Aeneas and prays for eternal enmity between her people and his. Then she sends her old nurse to fetch her sister; while the nurse is gone she mounts the pyre and draws a sword that had belonged to Aeneas, lets her thoughts dwell a moment on the memories of their love, and speaks her own epitaph, foundress of a noble city and great in achievement, happy if only he had never come into her life. Then she kisses the bed and stabs herself. In the uproar that follows her sister comes running and takes her in her arms. It is a little while before she dies.

When Aeneas not long afterwards has reached Italy and is taken by the Sibyl of Cumae down into the underworld to converse with his father's shade, he comes early in his passage through the infernal regions to the place assigned to those who have died through love. There in the half light he recognizes among other ghosts the ghost of Dido and speaks to her. He has heard of her death meanwhile, and knows that he has been the cause of it. He repeats his plea that he was not his own master: even so, he did not realize that the pain of his departure would drive her to this: this is the last time he can speak with her: must she turn away from him? Dido remains silent, her eyes fixed on the ground. Then suddenly she starts and hurries out of his sight into the shadows, where her husband Sychaeus waits, sharing her grief and loving her as she loves him. Aeneas looks with pity after her as she goes.

The last time that Dido is mentioned in the poem is near its end, when Aeneas takes leave of his young friend Pallas, killed in battle for his cause. He wraps the body in a robe of crimson and gold which Dido in the time of their love had made with her own hands for him.[6]

In producing the events outlined above three of the great gods of pagan mythology take a hand, all with different motives.[7] Juno, concerned to frustrate Aeneas' mission to re-found Troy, provokes the storm which drives Aeneas' fleet off course and brings him (not by her design) to the territory of Carthage. Jupiter, concerned for the safety of Aeneas in the interests of his mission, moves Dido to give the Trojans a kindly reception. Venus, concerned for Aeneas because he is her son, contrives that Dido shall become possessed with the fatal passion that ensures her misery. Juno, hoping to turn this development to account to keep Aeneas from Italy, contrives the fatal meeting in the cave which turns him from a guest into an openly acknowledged lover, and so creates a situation which cannot end except with Aeneas remaining permanently at Carthage as Dido's consort or his leaving her publicly humiliated as well as frustrated in her love. Jupiter, seeing that Aeneas is falling under the spell of Dido's powerful affection, now orders him abruptly to detach himself, and Dido is left in the situation which she presently terminates by suicide. What happens to Dido is thus—and this is one of the most terrifying aspects of the story—an accidental result of scheming and counter-scheming among the gods in which she is a pawn, an object not of hostility but of indifference. Yet she herself is wholly in their power. The obsessive love that seizes her is a demonic force, not an impulse which her will could have overcome. She tries at the beginning to resist, to be sure, and at the end she blames herself. But in fact, as the story is told, her will is not free, either at the banquet when she first falls in love, or in the encounter with Aeneas in the cave.

On the other hand her decision to kill herself when her love is faced with irrevocable frustration is the product of her own character and will in the circumstances that have arisen. She could have lived on, and seen from some points of view had much to live for. But she has lost not only the relationship which fills her life but all that she lived by before and gave up for it. Her respect for herself is marred by the failure of the resolution she had made to be true to the memory of Sychaeus and by the knowledge that she has been the slave and not the mistress of her desire. Her public honour is marred by the fact that she has flaunted her condition. Her pain in losing Aeneas can be measured by the account of her state before the fatal meeting in the cave, and it is made more bitter by the rejection which now attends it, and the rejection more bitter by being known to all.[8] Thus she combines the quality of a heroine of romance who dies for love when she is abandoned by her lover with that of a hero of tragedy who cannot live dishonoured and feels that only by death can he preserve the honour which he earned in his past life. The two feelings are expressed together in the words that she speaks as she is about to kill herself on the pyre amid the reminders of her lover. In these words the memory of their love is succeeded by the thought of Dido's past achievement: 'relics of a time so happy once, when fate and god allowed, receive my dying breath and free me from this anguish. I have lived my life and run the course that fate assigned me, and greatness will go with my spirit still to the world below. I founded a noble city. I saw stand walls that I made rise myself. I avenged my husband and punished the brother who was our enemy. Happy, too happy, if only the Trojan ships had never touched my shores.' The claim of achievement here is in the manner of epitaphs that Virgil knew, the epitaphs of the heroes of Roman history.[9]

The bitterness of Dido's tragedy is heightened in the telling in every possible way. The former life which she recalls in her final misery is brilliantly represented in the scenes of her first appearance in the story: the splendid temple, the throng of attendants, the queen beautiful and happy as she interests herself in the work of construction that is going on, and as she takes her seat on the throne of judgement with her royal guards at either hand; and then the sumptuous appointments of the palace in which she entertains her guests and hears, now doomed, the tale of Aeneas' past adventures.[10] The contrast between her kindness and its awful consequences for herself is pointed by Aeneas' prayer 'if the gods have any regard for human goodness, may heaven reward you worthily for this'.[11] The intensity of her suffering is pointed by the frivolity of the scenes in heaven, between Venus and Cupid and Juno, in which it is prepared. The break with Aeneas is contrived in the most painful and humiliating way for her by the accident which causes her to learn of his plans for departure before he tells her of them himself. The consequences add the bitterness of public and private shame to the pain of loss. The agony of her death when it comes is prolonged. Above all, the poet has communicated his feeling to the language of his narrative in an extraordinary degree, especially in his description of the growth of Dido's obsessive passion and of the formation of her resolve to die. He has also left the reader at the end acknowledging in Dido the heroic magnitude which she prized, and consoled with the parting glimpse of her reunion with Sychaeus.

It is a curious commentary on the story of Dido as it is told in the *Aeneid* that the original legend about her, which Virgil has drastically adapted, ran quite differently. In that legend Aeneas had no part, and Dido killed herself on the pyre to keep the faith which she had promised to the memory of Sychaeus, because she could not escape the suit of one of the neighbouring princes whom her people were pressing her to marry.[12]

In the evident symmetry of the poem's design the fate of Dido the lover is balanced by that of Turnus the rival. Both are victims of the destiny of Rome and Juno's opposition to it, and the Italian phase of the story ends in his death as the Carthaginian phase ends in hers.

We hear of Turnus first as a prince of high ancestry, favoured suitor for the hand of the Latin king's daughter. This he feels he has earned by his services to the Latins in their wars, and according to those who favour him he has had some assurances of it;[13] but the king has been warned by oracles not to give his daughter to any native of Italy but to await the coming of a destined husband for her from overseas. Turnus at first is unperturbed by the arrival of the Trojans in Italy; but an evil spirit sent by Juno rouses him to frenzied jealousy and anger. Calling his people to arms he marches to the Latin town, where meanwhile the Latin people have begun to clamour for war against the Trojans because of an affray (this too provoked by Juno's agent) in which Latin blood has been shed. Turnus thus becomes leader of the disaffected Latins as well as his own people, the Rutulians, and their allies from other parts of Italy. Encouraged by a message and sign from Juno he attacks the Trojan camp, while Aeneas is absent in search of allies for his own side, and is actually able to force his way into it. But he wastes his opportunity by his lack of self-control: instead of letting in his followers and capturing the camp he allows blood-lust to lure him into profitless slaughter at random until he is surrounded and driven out.[14] Now Aeneas returns to the scene, bringing allies with him from Etruria and from the Arcadian colony on the site of future Rome. Battle is joined, and Turnus kills in single combat the young Arcadian Pallas whose father has sent him with Aeneas to the war. He takes the young man's sword belt from his body as a trophy. On hearing of Pallas' death Aeneas is avid for revenge. But an encounter between him and Turnus at this stage is prevented by Juno, who lures Turnus off the battlefield in pursuit of a phantom Aeneas: Turnus chases the phantom on to a ship which is moored near by and which then slips its cable and carries him out to sea and finally home to his native city of Ardea. (This bizarre episode has not been fully worked into its context: it is treated afterwards as if it had never occurred.) With Turnus absent the Trojans gain the upper hand and the battle ends for that day.

A twelve-day truce now follows for the burial of the dead on both sides. During the negotiations Aeneas tells the Latin envoys that he is willing to settle the issue in single combat with Turnus but sends no formal challenge. Feeling against the war rises meanwhile in the Latin town and is inflamed by Turnus' political enemy Drances, who taunts Turnus with involving the people in war for his own

interest instead of fighting it out with Aeneas in a duel. Turnus
declares himself ready for this, but the debate at this point is broken
off by news that the enemy are approaching in force. Turnus goes
off to lay an ambush for the main army of the enemy, while a cavalry
action takes place on the plain in front of the town; in this the
Latins and their allies again have the worst of it, and Turnus on
receiving the news once more loses his opportunity through lack of
self-control; he abandons his ambush just before the enemy arrive at
the place, which they now pass safely by.[15]

Next day Turnus formally affirms his offer to meet Aeneas in single
combat. A truce is made accordingly. But Juno contrives for it to be
broken by the Italians, who are encouraged to this by a sign from
heaven. Aeneas is wounded by an arrow-shot in the confusion and
has to retire from the field. Turnus thinks he sees a chance of victory
and yields to the temptation to seize it. For a time he carries all
before him, until Aeneas returns into the battle, recovered from his
wound. Again the meeting of the two is for a time delayed, while
Turnus (kept out of his rival's way by Juno's agent the nymph
Juturna, who takes control of his chariot) pursues an illusion o
victory in a career of profitless slaughter. At last Aeneas turns his
attack on the city of the Latins and threatens it with capture.
Turnus on the other side of the plain is at first unaware. Then he
hears the ominous shouting in the distance. As he brings his chariot
to a halt his mood of exaltation subsides: he realizes that his success
has been an illusion, that he is defeated and has led his friends into
defeat: now if death awaits him he will die worthily of his ancestors.
A messenger, wounded, gallops up to tell him that the city is in
danger, the queen dead, the people talking of surrender. As he
stands dazed, his mind clouded by confused emotions, he sees fire
break out in the defence-works of the city: his mind clears and he
reaches a firm resolve, to go and face what he now knows will be his
death in combat with Aeneas. He hurries towards him and the two
face each other at last. They throw their spears without effect and
charge with their swords. Turnus' sword breaks in his hand as he
strikes: it is not his own but an inferior weapon seized in error
through his haste in setting out. Disarmed he runs before Aeneas
until Juturna comes to his help for the last time and gives him a
sword: Venus gives Aeneas back his spear: the two stand facing one
another again. In heaven the gods confer and Juno is persuaded to
abandon Turnus: Jupiter sends a bird of evil omen to chill his
spirit and as a sign to Juturna that she must abandon him too.

Turnus faces Aeneas' spear knowing that he is doomed; he heaves up a great stone to throw but feels his strength gone; the stone falls short; he stands helpless. Aeneas casts; the spear crashes through Turnus' shield and armour and transfixes his thigh; as he falls a great groan rises from the watching Italians. Turnus stretches out his hand in acknowledgement of defeat; he tells Aeneas to kill him if he will: he has deserved whatever comes to him. Aeneas pauses and is on the point of sparing his fallen enemy when his eye lights on the sword-belt that Turnus had taken from Pallas' body. Anger for his friend blazes up in him and he thrusts his sword into Turnus' heart. So the poem ends.

In this story, as in Dido's, the part of the gods is decisive. It is Juno who through her agents causes the Trojans to shed Latin blood, and compels the outburst of jealous anger in Turnus which rouses him to arms, and incites him to the attack on the Trojan camp which is the first act of open war. On the other hand Jupiter's will is shown working against Turnus in all that follows, to prevent him (through his own error) from capturing the camp and later from trapping Aeneas in his ambush, and to isolate and hamper and dishearten him in the duel between the rivals at the end. Juno meanwhile tries to delay his undoing by removing him from the battlefield after Pallas' death, and afterwards by sending Juturna to break the truce and to keep Turnus out of Aeneas' way in the subsequent fighting in pursuit of an illusory success. In all this she first dooms her own favourite and then shames him (for his words when the illusion leaves him show that that is how he feels it) by her efforts to delay the end for which she is responsible.[16] For she has known from the beginning that Aeneas' victory is certain, and it is in a last fit of revengeful pique that she thrusts Turnus into opposition to it. In the end she surrenders Turnus to his doom as part of her reconciliation with Jupiter and the destiny of Rome; only, as she says in her appeal to Juturna, she cannot bear to watch.[17]

Turnus, while his will is still his own, is unmoved by the effort of Juno's agent to inflame him against the newcomers at the beginning of the story. It is only when her supernatural power is directly asserted that he is filled with 'wild lust for battle and war's accursed frenzy and rage'.[18] Thereafter the terms repeatedly applied to him show that he is conceived as being in a state of furious excitement: he is *amens, turbidus, fervidus, ardens, furens, trepidans*, in a state of *insania* (madness), *furor* (frenzy), *violentia* (ungoverned passion).[19] The frequency of this last term, which is used of him alone in the

story, suggests that a passionate temper is conceived as his characteristic failing, as it is the characteristic failing of Achilles in the *Iliad*.
In battle he is twice at least shown as carried away by blood-lust,
and twice it is said that *furor* is the cause of his making a fatal tactical
mistake.[20] At the end of the story he is shown emerging from the
state of excitement in which he has been to the realization that he is
responsible for the defeat and death of those who have followed him.[21]
He tells Aeneas at the end that he has deserved to die if Aeneas
chooses to kill him. Dido too felt that she deserved to die. But their
sense of responsibility for the things that they have done does not
alter the fact that their wills originally have not been in their control.
Turnus like Dido has been the victim of a demonic possession. He
has also been deceived by his own piety. When Juno sends Iris as her
agent to incite him to attack the Trojan camp he recognizes her as a
goddess and acknowledges her divine authority with the same
reverent ritual observances as Aeneas uses in similar circumstances.
He is obeying here, as he begins the war, a direct command from
above.[22] He has no means of knowing that the war which he begins
is nevertheless 'an unholy war . . . thwarting the will of heaven'.[23]

It is apparent that Turnus is meant to have his share of the
reader's sympathy, fatally misguided though he is and bloodthirsty though he at times becomes in the heat of battle. Aeneas too
becomes bloodthirsty, and more grossly than Turnus, after the
death of Pallas. In particular, Turnus' act in taking the sword-belt
from Pallas' body is not to be construed as brutal or arrogant, any
more than the act of the famous Manlius Torquatus in taking the
torque from the Gaul.[24] Roman history abounded in stories in
which the taking of such trophies brought honour to those who took
them, and there is more than one other instance in the *Aeneid* itself.[25]
It is dramatically effective that the sword-belt should later become
the cause of Turnus' own death by re-awakening Aeneas' anger when
he is about to spare him; but the effect is one of poetic justice, not
of moral retribution. Turnus is no more conceived as an antipathetic
character than is Achilles in the *Iliad*. He has the affection of Latinus
as well as of his queen, and the esteem of his followers, to whom he
feels an honourable responsibility in his turn. He has evidently some
cause to feel that he has rights to the hand of the princess, though
the queen no doubt is exaggerating in reproaching Latinus with
'many promises'.[26] He has certainly cause to think of the Trojans
as aggressors, for in the affray with the Latins which Juno engineers
it is in fact the Trojans who draw first blood. When he is spoken of

as 'standing as champion of his native land', or calls on his men to 'stand in defence of Italy; drive the invaders from our land', he appears in a role which he can claim sincerely from his point of view and which Roman readers would not think unworthy.[27] At the end he goes to meet his death with a 'heroic' attitude not unlike that of Dido: he has erred and now in dying he will save his honour and 'go down a soul unstained, worthy to the end of my great ancestors'.[28] He is on the wrong side. But the contrast with the unattractive Drances, who is on the right side, leaves no doubt of the poet's sympathy with him as a human personality. In Juno's eyes he is *pius*, and *insons* (innocent).[29]

The fatal opposition of Dido and Turnus to the purpose of providence is associated in both of them with an ungovernable passion which excludes reason from the control of the will. This in Dido is desire, in Turnus rage, aroused by special circumstances in a character in which perhaps the tendency to excessive anger was always present. The same Latin word *furor* (or the related *furens* and *furiae*) is used repeatedly of both, a dozen times of Dido and half-a-dozen times of Turnus, to whom are also repeatedly applied the terms *violentia* and *violentus*. These words would suggest to Virgil's readers the destructive passions of the recent civil wars, the end of which is symbolized in Jupiter's prophecy in the first book of the *Aeneid* by the vision of *Furor* chained. Horace too, in the last of the *Odes*, a few years after Virgil's death, gives thanks that under Augustus *furor* and *vis* will never again banish the blessings of peace from Rome. Not long before, Cicero had used repeatedly in his denunciations of Antony the same combination of terms that characterize Turnus in the *Aeneid*, *violentus* and *furens*, *furor* and *violentia*.[30] These associations would necessarily attach to the destructive passions which ruin Dido and Turnus and bring ruin to their people too, to Dido's posterity through the curse in which she invokes the wars of Rome and Carthage and to Turnus' followers who fall in the war into which he leads them. Obviously in contrast to these passions stands the *pietas* of Aeneas and the disciplined humanity that it implies. But it would be a mistake to see in this the 'moral' of the *Aeneid*. As a moral it would be too obvious to need imparting, for everyone knows that it is better to be sane than mad. Moreover, it is in the essence of the experience of Dido and Turnus that they are ultimately the victims not of moral failure on their own part (though they feel this themselves) but of a conflict of purposes among powers in the world order which are overwhelmingly stronger than they.

V

THE HIGHER POWERS: FATE AND THE GODS

THE gods who so much affect the lives of Aeneas and Dido and
Turnus are depicted by the poet in human shape and with human
attributes, living and acting in human terms. This anthropomor-
phism is of course traditional, inherited ultimately from Homer and
sanctioned by long custom in literature and art. The resulting
anthropomorphic drama—though not all the details of it, some of
which are merely decorative—is necessary to the presentation of the
working of the divine powers in the story; it does not indicate that
the poet conceived the gods as having human form in reality. But
if his account of them is a fiction in this respect, it does not follow
that it is a fiction in all respects and that he does not believe, for
instance, in their existence, their plurality, their power, the diversity
of their wills, and the effect of these on the lives of human individuals.
He will not have supposed that the winds live in a cave in a mediterranean island, or that Neptune calms the sea with a trident, or that
Juno and Venus engage in angry altercations in a palace in the sky.
But this will not have prevented him from believing that there
existed divine powers which overthrew Troy, and could cause
storms or compass the deaths of Palinurus or Arruns, or inspire Dido
or Turnus with their fatal passions.[1] The belief in the reality of
supernatural powers and their working in the world is a separate
matter from the representations of them in art, as can be seen in
Homer when a god or spirit unidentified and so undepictable is
nevertheless felt by the people in the story to be at work, or in the
Aeneid when Evander senses, but cannot see, the presence of an
unidentified divinity on the hill which will later be the Capitol of
Rome.[2] Similarly an artist of Christian times who represents
Jehovah in a picture as a white-bearded human figure is likely to be
depicting a being in whose existence he believes under an aspect
which he knows to be fictitious.

Modern rationalism, impressed by the quaintness of the mythology surrounding the gods of Greece and Rome, and encouraged by
remarks such as Ovid's that 'it is expedient that there should be gods,
so let us fancy that there are',[3] may be tempted to suppose that

scepticism was general among the educated in Virgil's time. And scepticism no doubt was general about the myths; but not about the reality of supernatural forces. Until the impressive achievements of natural science in comparatively recent times there was far too much in the world that defied natural explanation to make scepticism of the supernatural anything but abnormal. But as beliefs about it were not regulated for the individual by an authoritative and intellectually organized theology, the form they took could vary greatly according to the temperament and experience of the believer. Given the traditional assumption of a plurality of powers, and the modifying influence of philosophical thought, and the tendency of his own feelings, the individual could form his own amalgam of ideas; which in any but the most rigorous thinker would be unlikely to be altogether self-consistent.

In Virgil's picture of the supernatural and its workings there is, to begin with, the concept of a fixed order of things, which we may call Fate. This includes on the one hand certain unalterable laws—for instance the mortality of human beings, and the period of suspense in limbo said to await the souls of the unburied after death: and on the other hand the unalterably predestined occurrence of certain events—for instance the fall of Troy, the union of Trojans and Latins to form a new race, the death of a Turnus or a Camilla in a certain war, the birth of Rome, the conquests of Rome, and so on. What Fate ordains is rigid and cannot be changed by power of god or prayer of man. But the texture, so to speak, of the ordinances of Fate is loose: much remains undetermined by it, and what is determined by it may sometimes be postponed though not averted. Thus, the fall of Troy to the Greeks was ordained by Fate but could have taken place as much as ten years later than it did.[4] The union of the Trojans and the Latins was ordained by Fate, but the name and language of the race to be derived from their union was not.[5] This conception of Fate and its operation has not of course been intellectually systematized. It reflects on the one hand a belief in the existence of Fate that is general and imprecise, and on the other hand an emotional conviction that this or that particular event is or was inevitable.

Co-existent with Fate are 'the gods'. These are individual powers with personal wills and purposes. But the will of one of them, Jupiter, is supreme over the rest, and is always identified with the ordinances of Fate. Whether he is author as well as executor of these ordinances is not always clear, and no doubt depends more on the poet's feeling in a given context than on any doctrinal theory.[6] Certainly under one aspect Jupiter in the *Aeneid* is a personification of Fate; and it results from this that the working of Fate in the poem appears as the working of a purpose and not simply as the fulfilment of an impersonal scheme: Fate assumes the character of Providence. Jupiter has however personal attributes independent of his identification with Fate. And his control over the other gods, though ultimately unquestioned, is intermittent in its application. Hence while he ensures the fulfilment of Fate's ordinances he also tolerates rather than prohibits the unsuccessful attempts which other gods sometimes make to frustrate them.

For in contrast with Jupiter the other gods, of whom there are many, are concerned only with the pursuit of independent purposes of their own. In their pursuit of these they cannot prevent what is laid down by Fate, though they may try to do so, with important incidental consequences. In the wide area of what is not ordained their wills have free scope, in so far as they do not impede one another. They may act without impinging on one another at all, or again they may co-operate, or conflict. There are moreover gradations of power among them: when Aeneas' wound in the final battle is miraculously healed by his mother Venus, acting unseen, the surgeon whose own efforts have been unsuccessful recognizes in the miracle the hand 'of one of the greater gods'.[7] The hierarchy extends downwards from the principal figures of the Greco-Roman Pantheon —Apollo, Neptune, Juno, Venus and the rest—to small divinities presiding over a locality or a special function, such as Portunus, who helps to victory in the ship-race the captain who prays to him at the crucial moment.[8] Where no greater god is concerned the will of a little god may be decisive. But a great god when he chooses will overrule a lesser: thus Neptune sends the Winds Eurus and Zephyrus packing from his premises in the storm scene at the beginning of the poem, and Venus at the end of it frees Aeneas' spear from the tree-stump in which Faunus has held it fast in answer to Turnus' prayer.[9] It sometimes happens that the gods are thought of as all agreed or all obedient to the will of their ruler Jupiter, and then 'the gods' will have the value of a collective power, an alternative term to Fate or Jupiter in describing the divine government of the world. But when their purposes are not harmonized, or are in conflict, or particular private purposes prevail, then the operation of the gods in the world will be random or arbitrary in its effect, perhaps even malevolent when an individual or nation is object of the hostility of particular powers.

Unlike Fate, the gods are, or may be, accessible to prayer and propitiatory worship. But the efficacy of prayer and worship is always uncertain, since the power concerned may be implacably offended, or indifferent, or prevented from effective response by an ordinance of Fate or the opposition of another deity. Piety will not ensure divine favour or preclude divine disfavour, any more than hard work and prudent calculation will necessarily ensure success or preclude failure in the business of life. But it will if consistently practised at least improve the chances that the person or nation that practises it will prosper under heaven. For this reason the Roman state was extremely careful in the management of its relations with the gods. It maintained a regular cycle of observances in their honour. It studied the signs by which their displeasure was thought to be manifested and took special measures to placate them when these occurred. It was at pains to seek evidence of their approval or disapproval when any important undertaking was contemplated. The victorious progress of Rome in history was naturally taken to show that the goodwill of the gods had in fact been promoted by these means; and in Virgil's day the traditional forms of national piety were being refurbished as an emotional assurance of the stability of Rome's greatness and the new order established at the end of the civil wars. Long afterwards the defenders of the traditional system against intellectual criticism—to which it was vulnerable, as having no theology and consisting in the maintenance of a set of rituals which were very ancient and in some cases very peculiar—came back again and again to the argument from results: the history of Rome was itself the proof that the Roman way of worshipping the gods was the way the gods themselves approved.[10]

This distinctively Roman attitude is reflected in the *Aeneid* in the conduct of the hero, who as leader of the Trojans is responsible for their relations with the gods, and for whom ritual and prayer are constant preoccupations. This can be seen in many contexts: on occasions of arrival and departure in the course of the Wanderings—in Thrace, at Delos, at Actium, at Castrum Minervae: after the vision of the Penates, and the ghost of Anchises, and the Tiber-god, and the sign given to Aeneas by Venus at Pallanteum, and the promise of the ships turned nymphs who greet his vessel as he approaches the battlefield: in the honours he pays to the dead—to his father, to Polydorus and Deiphobus, to Misenus and Caieta and Pallas: in the elaborate rituals preceding his descent into the underworld, and the truce with the Latins, and his dedication of Mezentius' armour.[11] Twice he is advised, and twice he obeys the advice, to pay exceptional honour to Juno his persecutress, and in the end the prayer he addresses to her at the making of the truce is granted when she abandons her opposition to his destiny and Rome's and accepts the promise of Jupiter that Romans will surpass all other nations in their reverence of herself.[12]

Thus it is not until the end of the *Aeneid* that the favour of the gods is assured to the Roman state and the hero of the poem who represents it. It is assured only after Aeneas has been subjected to long and severe tribulations because of Juno's hostility and has endured these patiently and been unremitting in his reverence and supplication towards his persecutor. 'Our commonwealth,' says Cicero, 'could never have attained its present greatness had it not laboured by every possible means to propitiate the immortal gods.'[13] But the favour of the gods thus eventually secured is not, in the *Aeneid*, the only or even the principal cause of the emergence of Rome; this emergence is ordained by Fate, the other component of the supernatural order, against which the opposition of individual gods could not in the last resort have prevailed. Thus at the end of the poem the whole of the supernatural order is seen as propitious to Rome. For the Roman state the higher powers are a benevolent entity, to which the Roman state has cause to give thanks.

But if we look away from the Roman state to the workings of Fate and the gods as they affect mankind in general, both individuals and nations, it is a strange and dismal picture that appears. The epithets that Virgil applies to Fate are at once instructive: *inexorabile* and *ineluctabile*.[14] This is no benign providence in his imagination but a power that is deaf to prayer and that holds a man in a grip of inevitability from which no struggling can avail him to escape. And the law of Fate, as we observe it illustrated in the scenes in the underworld in the sixth book of the poem, is harsh as well as inflexible. When Aeneas sees the souls of those whose bodies lie unburied doomed to roam in limbo for a hundred years before they can find rest, for no fault of their own, his mind is troubled and he 'pities the injustice of their lot'; and when Palinurus begs to be delivered, the Sibyl rebukes his importunity with the warning 'not to hope that the ordinances of god can be altered by prayer'.[15] Such is Aeneas' first encounter with a soul in the world of the dead. His last is when he sees the spirit of Marcellus, unborn as yet but doomed already to an untimely death, and Anchises exclaims in grief 'o that he could break the cruel bond of fate'.[16] The order imposed on the world by Fate is a grim and harsh one, with nothing in it to satisfy the moral instincts of man. Nor does it restrain the multiplicity of individual divine powers, the gods, from making him their plaything or their victim. ·

Of these powers as they appear in the *Aeneid* none except Jupiter is motivated by anything but private interests and affections. Thus Venus is concerned for Aeneas because he is her son; Neptune for his rights as monarch of the sea; Vulcan for the satisfaction of his amorous desires; Cybele for the pine-trees, now ships, which once stood in her grove; Diana for her favourite Camilla; and Juno, incessantly, for her grievance against Troy and ambitions for her own city of Carthage.[17] The point here is not that the gods' purposes are always bad, but that they are essentially private. Sometimes they are innocuous. Sometimes they are callous, as when Venus inspires in Dido a love which she knows is bound to be frustrated. Often they are malevolent, as when Juno provokes the storm, the burning of the ships, the war in Italy, the attack on the Trojan camp. Moreover, in pursuit of their purposes the gods do not hesitate to exploit the reverence of men for them as a means of deceiving men to their own harm. When Laocoon warns the Trojans not to trust the offering of the Wooden Horse the gods, who are planning the destruction of Troy, discredit his warning by sending a fearful visitation against himself. When Iris incites the Trojan women to set fire to the ships she is recognized as a goddess and as such obeyed. When she incites Turnus to attack the Trojan camp she is recognized and obeyed in the same way. An elaborately contrived omen deceives the Latins into believing that the general will of heaven is with them when they break the truce which their king has just solemnly concluded.[18] Thus in its total effect the divine power in its dealings with men appears as irresponsible and heartless. And the pathos of man's dependence in consequence is illustrated in more than one scene of fruitless entreaty. The Trojans are giving thanks for their supposed deliverance at the temples of the gods at the very moment when the gods are preparing their destruction. Aeneas prays that the gods may reward Dido worthily for her kindness just as they are about to reward her with misery and shame. Dido herself at the banquet with which she makes her visitors welcome prays that Jupiter, who enjoins and presides over the duty of hospitality of man to man, may cause this to be a day of happy memory for her guests and her own people and their posterity, when it is in fact to be the beginning of ruin for herself and hers. Later in the depth of her agony she prays for the help of 'whatever power in heaven is merciful and just', in vain.[19] Repeatedly in the story a victim of the gods is *insons* or *immeritus*, or his fate *iniquus*. Troy's fall was 'undeserved', yet it pleased the gods to bring it about. Turnus is 'innocent', but doomed to die. Dido's fate is 'cruel' and 'unjust'. Palinurus is 'guiltless', but a god engineers his death, and Fate, because his body is unburied, denies repose to his soul: a sufficiently grim illustration of the way of god and Fate alike with man.[20] Dido and Turnus, as we have seen, are thrust by a god into conflict with Fate and broken in the result.

The *Aeneid* thus reflects a feeling about the supernatural which on the one hand is congenial to Roman national sentiment and vindicates the religious system of the Roman state but on the other hand is profoundly discouraging to the individual. The *Aeneid* is sometimes referred to as a religious poem, but perhaps it would be better described as a document of religious history. For the feeling that pervades it cannot have been peculiar to the poet; it must be one that he shared with others in the world in which he lived. It will not of course have been universal. On the one hand there existed intellectual systems such as that of the Epicureans, who excluded supernatural agencies from any influence on the course of events, or that of the Stoics, who conceived the whole world as subject to a single controlling purpose, benign in its nature, and admitted separate divinities only as aspects of this or subordinate agents.[21] On the other hand, for the great majority who did not adhere to such systematic doctrines the inherited ideas of the divine, confused as they were and unregulated by any organized theology, admitted many varieties of belief and feeling according to the temperament and experience of the individual. We read on the one hand of extremes of superstitious anxiety; and on the other hand we can detect often enough, as we should expect, an attitude that assumes that if a man leads a normally decent life and pays the gods normal respect he need no more live in fear of them than the average man nowadays lives in fear of accident or grave disease, though he knows that such misfortunes may occur. No doubt many people felt in some degree protected by the deities of the household with whom they had a certain intimacy, the Lares who watched Tibullus play as a child and to whom he prays when he is going to the war, or the domestic Jupiter to whom Juvenal gives thanks for the return of his friend.[22] But there are clear indications that to many the supernatural was a source of fear rather than comfort, and especially the arbitrary and the inexorable elements in its working. This is shown by the missionary character of the Epicurean philosophy, which regarded the fear of the supernatural as a principal cause of human unhappiness, and which became fashionable at Rome about the beginning of Virgil's life-time. In Lucretius' poem *De Rerum Natura*, which is the principal document of Latin Epicureanism and which appeared about thirty years before the *Aeneid*, the fear of the gods is a fear of the wanton and arbitrary action on human life of powers that are cruel and easily offended, or, as appears in one striking passage, of *a* power, mysterious and unpredictable, which is as it were the sum of all of these, and which seems to be at work all the time 'crushing and trampling on the lives of men and making them its playthings'.[23] This is the power elsewhere called Fortune, an abstraction of the chaotic working of the divine in the world, which came in the Hellenistic age to be endowed with personality and worshipped as a goddess, irrational and so capricious, and callous and cruel in the exercise of her caprice: 'plying her cruel art with glee and never tiring of her wanton sport'.[24] Fortune appears in the *Aeneid* too as a power behind the perversity of the gods or the inexplicable ways of fate: she represents the arbitrary element in the working of the divine. But to the founder of Epicureanism the inevitable was not less dreadful than the arbitrary as enemy of human peace of mind: 'it would be', he said, 'better to accept the fables about the gods than to be a slave to the determinism of the scientists'.[25] In this he has in mind the determinism of a mechanical chain of causation rather than that of a conscious supernatural will. But the reason why either is alarming is the same: that man is left in the grip of an *inexorable* power.

That the fears which Epicurus hoped to dispel by his philosophy were persistent and widespread in the Graeco-Roman world can be seen from a document of the generation immediately following Virgil's own. The elder Pliny describes in his *Natural History* three beliefs about the powers which govern the universe that he says were commonly current in his day.[26] The first of these supposes a multiplicity of separate divinities, potentially unlimited, and easily leads those who hold it into extravagances of superstition. The second identifies in the working of the supernatural in the world a power which is essentially arbitrary and irrational, and worships this as a goddess under the name of Fortune, 'fickle and changeable and patroness of the unworthy'. The third excludes both gods and Fortune from the government of man's affairs and holds that what happens to each of us in life is determined by the star under which he is born: that is to say, believes in the kind of impersonal determinism which is the basis of astrology, a determinism not less grim than other kinds, since a cog in a clockwork mechanism is as helpless as a pawn at the disposal of the purpose of a chess-player. Thus the people of whom Pliny speaks, and whom he implies (though he does not share any of their beliefs) to be the majority of men, see the world as governed by powers chaotic, or arbitrary, or inexorable: by the confused purposes of innumerable gods, or by Fortune, or by Fate. If we now look forward over two centuries to the *Metamorphoses* of Apuleius, we find that these beliefs are still typical, and that to liberate men from the terrors that attend them is the merit of a new kind of religion. The goddess Isis, to whose worship the hero of the *Metamorphoses* is converted, is conceived as incorporating in her single person the powers of all the gods of paganism and applying them with benevolence to the comfort and protection of those who entrust themselves to her. In a remarkable passage it is said of her that she 'keeps men from harm by land and sea, and gives shelter in life from storm and stress, and stretches out the hand that saves, and unwinds the tightly twisted strands spun by the Fates, and calms the tempests of Fortune, and halts the baneful motions of the stars'.[27] Here Fortune and Fate and the Stars are powers that men fear and long to escape, and Isis is a saving power that masters them. 'I am stronger than Fate; Fate is obedient to my will' runs a passage in an Isiac hymn.[28] But the mass of men, who have not found their way to the protection of Isis, remain at the mercy of powers formidable and often cruel. The promise of the new kind of religion is evidence of the terrors of the old.

It will be seen from this that the *Aeneid* is in an important sense representative of the feelings widespread in Virgil's world about the supernatural powers. It is a confused and dismal picture. But however arbitrary and harsh may be the working of the divine order in general, it is consistent and benevolent towards the Roman state; and whatever the fears and doubts of the individual on his own account, as a citizen he can be confident and grateful that the nation of which he is a part stands under the protection of heaven.

There appears also for a moment in the poem the figure of a god who has been once a man, whose character it is to come to the help of men and free them from terrors that beset them. Such were Castor and Pollux, protectors of sailors, under whose sign was the ship of Alexandria which brought St. Paul from Malta to Puteoli on his way to Rome. Such also was Hercules, whose labours had come to be conceived as a purging of the world from robbers and monsters for the good of human kind, and to whom Evander and his Arcadians are sacrificing when Aeneas comes to them in quest of their alliance.[29] 'To us also in the fullness of time,' says Evander to his guest, 'there came a god at last to help us in our need.'[30] Thus there glimmers in the background the hope of a saviour god.

VI

PRINCIPLES OF STRUCTURE: CONTINUITY AND SYMMETRY

THE *Aeneid* combines a great variety of subject-matter with a satisfying unity of total effect. Three of the sources of this unity of effect are indicated already in the prologue to the poem, and have been the subject of earlier chapters of this book. First there is the grand theme: *tantae molis erat Romanam condere gentem* (1.33). Secondly there is the person of the hero who gives his name to the *Aeneid.* Thirdly there is the poet's sense, pervading his work, of the unhappy mystery of the ways of the higher powers with man: *tantaene animis caelestibus irae?* (1.11). There remains a fourth element to be considered, the nature of the unity of the poem's structure.

The literary fashion current in Virgil's youth favoured the example of certain Greek poets of the Hellenistic age whose preferred unit of composition was a piece of close texture and relatively brief compass: the didactic monograph, the idyll, the narrative episode.[1] If a longer work came to be, it was in essence a collection of short ones. Virgil's own poetry, before the *Aeneid*, was of this kind. The *Eclogues* are a collection of ten pieces of an average length of less than a hundred lines. The *Georgics* are a collection of four pieces of an average length of rather more than five hundred lines. It is easy to imagine that the construction of an epic presented a considerable problem to a poet with this background, and that his past tastes and experience would be likely to be reflected in his solution of it.

It was observed earlier that the *Aeneid* is the first chapter of a much longer story, the story of Rome, rather than itself a complete story with an end of the kind defined by Aristotle as 'that after which nothing naturally is'.[2] The *Aeneid* at its end leaves the reader with a strong feeling that much still remains to be told. It is also apparent that the *Aeneid* is far from having the 'single action' which according to Aristotle should unify an epic just as it should a tragedy,[3] but includes on the contrary two separate 'actions', well-defined in that the scenes of them are set in Carthage (Books 1–4) and in Italy (Books 7–12) respectively and that the interest in each is focused on the experience of a secondary hero of its own. These two actions are the most conspicuous feature of the structure of the poem, but do not by any means account for the whole of its content. The fifth and sixth books stand between them and belong to neither; the second and third books are parenthetic in the action which is set at Carthage. The action set in Italy is diversified with numerous and various episodes on which an element of plot has been only superficially imposed. It is noticeable also how often an individual book is a self-contained segment of material: the fall of Troy, the wanderings of the Trojans, the descent of Aeneas into the underworld, the attack on the Trojan camp. In the last book of the poem an effect of artistic unity is sought by bringing together two motives which in the *Iliad* are separated by seventeen books—the challenge and abortive truce at the beginning and the duel in earnest at the end.* From all this one derives the impression that the *Aeneid* is an edifice built up of shorter units which have been carefully constructed as such themselves. The question is, on what principle was the building done?

Basically the story consists of a sequence of trials and difficulties encountered by the Trojans in wandering and war over a period of seven years, from the fall of Troy to their final victory in Latium. It could have been narrated as a simple chain of episodes, as Apollonius of Rhodes in his *Argonautica* narrated the adventures of the Argonauts on their way to and from Colchis to bring back the Golden Fleece. But Virgil has imposed a pattern, or rather a succession of patterns, on his material by means adopted from the Homeric poems. From the *Odyssey* he has taken the idea of the retrospect, the narrative within the story of events that took place before its formal beginning;† this breaks up the linear sequence of the tale of the wanderings and procures (in combination with the personal story of Dido) the well-defined unit of Books 1–4 with which the poem starts. From the *Iliad* he has taken the idea of an action divided into two parallel courses and later reunified which governs the layout of the story of the war in Latium in Books 7–12.‡ From the *Iliad* he has also taken the motive of the death of the hero's friend at the hand of the enemy champion, and the hero's quest for vengeance and

---

* The truce and breaking of the truce from *Iliad* 3 and 4; the final duel from *Iliad* 22.

† In the *Odyssey*, the hero narrates the story of his past adventures, in Books 9–12, to the king and queen of the Phaeacians, in whose country he has been cast up after shipwreck in a storm.

‡ In the *Iliad*, as in the *Aeneid*, the hero is removed from the scene of combat, and in his absence the enemy come near to winning a decisive success. In both poems the hero's reappearance then leads to the dénouement.

achievement of it after initial frustrations, which provides the latter part of the war story with an element of plot.* The results of this for the structure of the *Aeneid* are principally two. First, the sequence of events is sophisticated instead of simple in the narration both of the wanderings and of the war. Secondly, the narratives of the wanderings and the war emerge as two well-defined units embracing Books 1–4 and 7–12 respectively, the latter with a rather strong punctuation internally at the point where the divided action in it (divided in 8 and 9) is reunified at the beginning of Book 10.

The character of the groups 1–4 and 7–12 as planned units of composition is marked very clearly, not only by the fact that each has its own location and its own sub-hero—Carthage and Dido in the one case, Latium and Turnus in the other—but also by the fact that the action in each is begun by an intervention of Juno (preceded in each case by a soliloquy in similar terms) and ends with the death of the sub-hero in the final line.[4] In between, Books 5 and 6 make a transition from wanderings to war: Book 5 brings the last hazard of the wanderings, the firing of the ships by the mutinous women; Book 6 brings the travellers to Italy and announces that the wanderings are over, while it also foreshadows the coming war:[5] the two at the same time are linked together by the person of Aeneas' dead father Anchises, who is honoured by his son with the funeral games in Book 5 and the descent (made for the father's sake) into the underworld in Book 6, and is conceived throughout as furnishing him with inspiration and encouragement. The resulting division of the poem into groups of four and two and six books may have been suggested (like the device of the retrospective narrative of the hero's adventures) by the *Odyssey*, the twenty-four books of which are divided into groups of four and eight and twelve. It seems likely that an instinct for proportion is at work here. It is in any case surely a mistake to think of the *Aeneid* as consisting, in any important sense, of two equal halves. The design of the poem is intended to avoid this, just as it is intended to avoid a naïvely linear sequence of events.

In the scheme discussed above the longest unit is the last (Books 7–12), and it contains the part of the *Aeneid* story which is a story of war. This corresponds to the ancient idea that war, with its heroic associations, was the 'highest' subject, the one that demanded most

* The Arcadian prince Pallas, killed by Turnus, corresponds in this respect to Patroclus, killed by Hector in the *Iliad*. The story of Pallas' feats and death is told in *Aeneid* 10.362–509; the rage of Aeneas on his account, in 10.510–604; the mourning for him, and his funeral procession, in 11.29–99 and 139–81; the final vengeance of Aeneas on the killer, in 12.697–952.

of a poet's powers and evoked the greatest poetry if those powers were adequate to respond to the challenge. Epic poetry was poetry at its greatest; and the characteristic of the epic poet was to write 'of warring kings' or 'of battles and the fall of cities'.[6] Hence the beginning of the tale of war in the *Aeneid* is heralded by the announcement: 'I will tell of grim war and battles and princes driven by their passions to their deaths, and the armies of Etruria, and all Italy assembled under arms. A vaster story now begins for me, a vaster theme I take in hand.'[7] This certainly was the poet's mind; whether it corresponded to his natural feelings is another matter.

The methods of design so far considered have related chiefly to the evolution of the story, the way in which the poet has set out the progress of the hero towards his goal through trial, temptation and hazards of war. There is however another principle of design also at work in the *Aeneid*, a kind of symmetry, which one might call architectural, in the disposition of certain elements of the material. For instance, the fates of Dido and Turnus are in some evident ways parallel to one another; and in addition to this, there is a very close parallelism between the scenes which begin the two actions which lead to their respective deaths—the soliloquy and intervention of Juno that initiates the storm in Book 1 and the similar soliloquy and intervention that initiates the war in Book 7. The two actions are unequal in length and represent successive stages of a developing story. At the same time they match one another, in a kind of congruence that is not of quantity but of motif. Two different principles of composition, not necessarily incompatible, are at work.

Another conspicuous parallelism is that between the pageant of future Alban and Roman heroes whom Aeneas sees as unborn souls in the underworld at the end of Book 6 and the pageant of scenes from future Roman history which are depicted on the god-made shield brought to him by his mother Venus at the end of Book 8. The recurrence, in these passages, of the pageant-movement and of the prophetic vision of Rome as end to which all the story of the poem is tending makes a repetition of motif that must be deliberate; and this may prompt us to look further at the context in which it occurs. The bringing of the shield to Aeneas is preceded by a scene in which Venus appeals to Vulcan for his help and Vulcan is seen at work in his smithy, with his Cyclops assistants, on the arms that he has promised.[8] This corresponds to a scene at the end of Book 5 in which Venus appeals to Neptune to ensure Aeneas a calm and safe passage from Sicily to Italy and so a final end to the hazards of the wanderings; whereupon Neptune is seen riding in his chariot over the sea, attended by nymphs and lesser sea-gods, and quieting the winds and waves.[9] Here again the motif (the appeal of Venus to a fellow-Olympian for help for Aeneas, and the scene of the Olympian's activity in response) is distinctive, and the fact of a repetition accordingly evident. Nor is this all. The journey of Aeneas in Book 8 to Pallanteum (which he has prolonged into Etruria when he later receives the Vulcan-made arms from his mother) is brought about by a dream in which the Tiber-god appears to him and quiets the anxiety aroused in him by the threat of war.[10] In the same way the descent of Aeneas into the underworld in Book 6 (where he sees the vision of future Roman heroes) is brought about by a dream in which his father appears to him and quiets the anxiety aroused in him by the mutiny of the women in Sicily and their attempt to set the ships on fire.[11] Here again motif, context and function are all common to the two events and again the fact of a repetition is evident. It results that in each of these two sections of the story (5.700–6.901 and 8.1–731) there is the same sequence of distinctive motifs: the comforting dream which prompts the ensuing action, the successful appeal of Venus to a fellow-Olympian for help for her son, and the prophetic pageant of future Roman history. Between the sections of narrative paired by this repeated sequence two things have happened, the arrival of the Trojans at their journey's end in Latium (7.1–285) and the first stirrings of war against them at Juno's instigation (7.286–817). These two themes are interwoven in what follows. For while Aeneas' quest for allies in Book 8 arises from the war situation, it is in its content a part of the story of arrival at journey's end, bringing the hero as it does to the site of future Rome, and having as it does a peaceful and auspicious atmosphere. In fact, the arrival in Italy in Book 6 (with the scenes preparatory to this at the end of Book 5) and the arrival at the site of Rome in Book 8 are parts of a complex in which the outbreak of war is less significant immediately than the signs of welcome and divine favour which attend the Trojans' coming to their appointed destination. The actual moment of this is in Book 7, and is marked by the sign of the 'eaten tables', confirmed by a triple roll of thunder from the sky in answer to Aeneas' prayer.[12] Meanwhile we have learned that prophecies have warned the native people of the land to expect the coming of a man of destiny, and in the following exchange of speeches between the Trojan envoys and the Latin king the envoys' declaration that 'divine revelations of destiny have commanded us

I V A—E

to seek this land of yours' is answered by the king with the surmise that 'he, your leader, is as I believe the man called for by the fates'.[13] It is surely not without significance that this exchange takes place in a building in the Latin city so described—as was remarked earlier, in Chapter II—that it must seem an anticipation of the great temple of Jupiter on the Capitol in historical Rome: set on a hill, itself a tall edifice with many columns, adorned with spoils of war, with statues of former kings and heroes at its doors, at once a temple and a council-chamber, scene of ritual banquets, scene of the investiture of each new ruler with the symbols of his office's authority.[14] This moment is preceded and followed by sign after sign of divine favour and reassurance: the golden bough, to be plucked only by him who is called by fate, the 'eaten tables', the triple thunder-clap, the sow with thirty young, the flash of arms in the sky and the trumpet-blast that announces the coming of Venus with the promised panoply.[15] In this phase of the story, moreover, the progress of the Trojans from Sicily to Italy, from Cumae to the Tiber-estuary, from Tiber estuary to the site of Rome, is assisted at each stage by miraculous calm of sea and river; and this progress leads to Rome as if symbolically of the meaning of the whole poem.[16] Thus the repetition of the same sequence of motifs in Book 6 (with 5.700–871) and Book 8 serves to demarcate and to emphasize an area of the poem which has a special significance, and this significance is in fact indicated by the repeated motifs—reassurance of the call of destiny, divine aid, and the prophetic vision of Rome.

Between the Carthaginian episode of Books 1–4 and the arrival of the Trojans in Italy comes the story in 5.1–699 of the games held in Sicily for Anchises and the mutiny of the women, related to both and yet distinct. Between the arrival of Aeneas at the site of Rome and his appearance on the battlefield at the beginning of Book 10 comes the attack on the Trojan camp in his absence in Book 9, again related to the previous and the following phases and yet distinct, for the hero is wholly absent from it. In these two widely separated episodes of the poem there is again a repetition of a clearly identified motif, indicating presumably some kind of a correspondence between them in the poet's mind. In Book 5 Juno sends Iris as her agent to provoke the women to mutiny. In Book 9 Juno sends Iris to incite Turnus to attack the camp in Aeneas' absence.[17] In both cases what follows is an attempt to set fire to the Trojan ships. The nature of the correspondence in the poet's plan between the two portions of the poem marked by this repetition is made plain by the prevalence in them of repetitions of another kind. Mnestheus, a captain distinguished in the ship-race at the games, is also a deputy commander of the camp in Aeneas' absence, and he distinguishes himself again now in heartening the defenders as he earlier heartened his crew in the race. Nisus and Euryalus, principal figures in the foot-race at the games, are heroes of the nocturnal adventure, fatal to themselves, which makes an episode in the defence of the camp. Above all, Ascanius, heir of Aeneas and eponymous ancestor of the Roman Julii and so of Octavian-Augustus, is seen in both these contexts distinctively in the role of a future leader. In Book 5 he is captain of the young Trojans who exhibit their horsemanship at the games, and is first to confront and appeal to the women who have set fire to the ships; in Book 9 he shares the command in the camp with his senior advisers, and in the action himself shoots down an enemy champion who has been taunting the defenders. The correspondences of repeated motif between these two parts of the poem thus reflect a correspondence of function of these parts in its economy: they both allow a momentary prominence on the scene to Trojan characters other than Aeneas.[18]

The presence of this elementary yet elaborate system of correspondences in the structure of the *Aeneid* may seem strange, but the facts are there and admit no explanation but intention on the part of the poet. That Virgil had an inclination towards this sort of pattern-making can be seen from the disposition of the components in his two collections, the *Eclogues* and the *Georgics*. The first nine *Eclogues* are arranged in such a way that the first and ninth, second and eighth, third and seventh, fourth and sixth are paired respectively by evident common characteristics—personal allusion, the subject of love, the form of a poetic contest, movement away from the pastoral. The four *Georgics* are disposed in two pairs, each pair with its own prologue and each individual piece with its own epilogue, the epilogues being so treated that each pair exhibits a similar movement of feeling. But an epic story is a very different matter from a collection of separate pieces, and it may well be asked how this kind of pattern-making can be contrived in a continuous narrative without distorting the natural course of it or complicating the poet's task beyond endurance. The answer is that this is easy in the *Aeneid* because of the episodic character of the poem. It is, in one sense, a chequer-work of episodes, some of which are unessential to the development of the story that runs through them. In fact, the effects of symmetry identified above in the area covered by Books 5–9 of the *Aeneid* could all be produced by selecting material to compose Books 5 and 6—in which the evolution of the story proper makes no demands at all—with an eye to correspondences with the contents of Books 8 and 9. It is reported in the best of the ancient Lives of Virgil[19] that he made a plan of the whole *Aeneid* in prose before beginning to compose it as a poem, and this procedure itself would favour, though not of course require, a system of design such as the correspondences imply.

There remains the question, what was the object of this procedure. Some of the repetitions can be seen to afford a wanted emphasis: for instance the prophetic pageants, or the double appearance of Ascanius in an obviously significant role. But in others the repetition can be nothing but a part of a pattern-making process: for instance the double sending of Iris by Juno, the double firing of the ships, the two similarly encouraging and action-prompting dreams, the two solicitations of her peers by Venus on her son's behalf (which themselves appear to be counterparts to the two interventions of Juno against him). The pattern adumbrated by the repetitions (or groups of repetitions) in Books 5–9 converges to the centre of the poem, with its anticipations of Rome in the first meeting of the representatives of Troy and Latium—the obviously symbolic significance of the moment, the promise of joint destiny acknowledged in the speeches of both parties, and the foreshadowing of the Roman Capitol in the building in which the meeting takes place—and it may be that there is an intention to frame, as it were, the image of Rome in this position as the true subject of the story. But we must reckon also more generally with the instinct to impose shape and order on material which lacks the unifying influence of a plot of the Aristotelian kind. In other words, the poet may be resorting, in this part of the designing process, to a principle of construction that is really architectural rather than literary. The lines of this are not obtrusive, and are probably meant to be felt more than seen. Similarly, the skeleton gives shape to the human person, but the beauty of the human person is not best appreciated in an X-ray photograph. An analysis such as that undertaken in the present chapter may yield some lessons helpful to the understanding of the *Aeneid*, but it can be and perhaps should be forgotten when these have been absorbed.

The combination of elements of symmetry with a narrative progress need not surprise us. It can be seen for instance in Catullus' sixty-fourth poem, the tale of the wedding of Peleus and Thetis, in which the story of Ariadne and Theseus is told as a description of a figured tapestry on the marriage bed. The description begins with Ariadne on the shore of Naxos and Theseus' ship departing in the distance, and ends with Ariadne on the shore and Bacchus approaching to console her.[20] Within this frame the poet narrates the story of Ariadne and Theseus and its sequel for Theseus in two matching chapters disposed symmetrically about a further description, central to the whole composition, of Ariadne alone and disconsolate, lamenting her betrayal.[21] The same principle can be seen at work in a less elaborate way in the account of the fall of Troy in the second book of the *Aeneid* itself. There the desperate resistance of Aeneas in the first confusion and his escape through the contrasting silence after resistance has ceased are narrated in passages which frame the central scene of the storming of Priam's palace and in turn are framed by the descriptions of the apparition of Hector which begins the whole episode and the apparition of Creusa which concludes it. Again, the poet of the *Iliad* has sought a kind of symmetry in the framing of the long story of the fighting (Books 2–22) between the preliminaries in the first two books (1–2) and the aftermath in the last two (23–24); and in the composition of the series of episodes which make up the first day's fighting (3–7); and in the evident correspondence of the two abortive duels (in 3 and 7) which begin and end the first day's fighting with the two duels in earnest (in 16 and 22) which enclose the final phase. Another instructive example is Milton's *Paradise Lost*, in which the events leading up to Satan's frustrated attempt (in Book 4) to corrupt Adam and Eve and the events following his later successful attempt (in Book 9) are separated, like the two attempts themselves, by the four-book-long conversation (5–8) between Adam and Raphael which fills the middle of the poem and recounts all that has happened before the action of the poem began. On the three-fold division of the poem thus produced there is then imposed a two-fold division of a different kind. For the conversation of Adam and Raphael (5–8) is in two parts, of which the first recounts the fall of the angels and the second the creation of our world. This second part of the conversation (in 7–8) is contrived to make a continuum with the main narrative of the poem when this is resumed (in 9). As a result the second half of the poem (7–12) contains a continuous narrative of the history of this world from the creation, and this is marked by the poet at the beginning of Book 7 with the words 'half yet remains unsung . . .'. Thus a division of the poem into three parts (1–4, 5–8 and 9–12) on one principle is combined with a division into two parts (1–6 and 7–12) on another. In the *Aeneid* also, though in a different way, two principles of composition are simultaneously at work. On the one hand, there is the evident division of the story into a series of acts or stages corresponding to its progress: the adventure at Carthage (1–4); the last stage of the wanderings (5–6); the war in Italy (7–12), which in turn divides into the outbreak of war (7–9) and the final conflict (10–12). On the other hand, there is a symmetrical disposition of episodes in the central part of the poem (5–9), apparently centring on, and so emphasizing, the moment at the beginning of Book 7 when the Trojans arrive at their new home in Italy. In all this part of the poem the idea of Rome as subject of the whole story is insistently presented to the reader's mind—by repeated mention of the name of Rome, by the introduction into the story of anticipations of characteristically Roman institutions, by the adaptation of famous Homeric episodes in such a way as to give them a specifically Roman significance, by signs prophetic of the coming of Rome, by revelations of Rome's future history, and by bringing the hero to the very site of future Rome itself.[22] This Roman theme is developed especially in Books 6–8, which recount the arrival of the Trojan immigrants successively in Italy, in Latium and at the site of future Rome. In the two books, 5 and 9, which stand between this story of the arrival (6–8) and the end of the preceding Carthaginian episode (1–4) on the one hand and the beginning of the final conflict (10–12) on the other, there is apparent an intention on the part of the poet to diversify his story by giving a number of secondary characters on the Trojan side a chance to occupy briefly the centre of the stage. This elaborate construction in the middle part of the poem is possible because of the episodic character of most of the material composing it. To feel the effect of it is more important than to be aware of the fact of it: and the division of the poem on which the reader's awareness needs to be focused is that marking the stages (or acts) which carry the progress of the story, namely Books 1–4, 5–6 and 7–12 (with its internal subdivision into 7–9 and 10–12).

VII

POETIC EXPRESSION: LANGUAGE AND SENSIBILITY

THE elements of the *Aeneid* that have been the subject of the preceding chapters—the central theme, the experience of the principal characters, the design and architecture of the whole—these are all necessary ingredients of an epic story. But an epic story need not be an epic poem, and Virgil was a poet before he was an epic poet. A book about the *Aeneid* must therefore include some consideration of the properties that distinguish the poet from other kinds of literary artist. But poetry in this sense, the poetry of diction, resists analysis, because it is something different from the sum of its components, and because its components in any case are not measurable nor all identifiable. It cannot therefore be described or explained. All that can be done is to comment on some selected characteristics of it of which a reader can profitably be aware.

Virgil's diction, though it shares to a great extent the vocabulary and usage of contemporary prose, is designedly a 'poetic' diction, as for instance is the diction of *Paradise Lost* or the *Idylls of the King*. Thus, the vocabulary is marked by a sprinkling of words and phrases inherited from earlier poetry or formed on analogy of it; archaic forms such as *olli, aquai, fuat, vixet* (additional and alternative to *illi, aquae, sit, vixisset*); compounds of a type obsolete in the Latin of the poet's own time, such as *velivolus, vulnificus, horrisonus, letifer, fatifer, laniger, saetiger*; alternatives, such as *fari, gemini, longaevus, superi, planta, palma, mucro, cuspis, genitor, natus, germanus* for common words such as *dicere, duo, senex, dei, pes, manus, gladius, hasta, pater, filius, frater*, and a long series of variant terms for 'sea'—*altum, sal, pelagus, pontus, aequor, marmor, gurges, undae, freta, vada*, as well as *mare* itself. A good deal of this 'poetic' vocabulary has its counterpart in the English poetic diction current in the eighteenth and nineteenth centuries; in 'thou' and 'ye', for instance, and 'mine' = 'my', and 'had' = 'would have', and 'quoth' and 'spake' and 'twain' and 'aged' and 'blade' and 'sire', to say nothing of 'deep', 'brine', 'main', 'billows', etc. This element of vocabulary colours Virgil's diction but does not dominate it. Nor does it result in quaintness or affectation:

for a diction differing in this way from that of prose seemed both to the poet and to his public—who turned to poetry for their pleasure as naturally as a modern reader turns to the novel—to be the natural and appropriate medium for an epic poem, distinguished from common speech as the world of the epic is removed from the world of everyday. It accords with this that from time to time Virgil echoes a whole phrase or group of words from his great predecessor in Latin epic, Ennius. Such are *est locus, Hesperiam . . .*; *summa . . . opum vi*; *olli . . . respondit*; *sancte deorum*; *belli ferratos postes*; *omnes arma requirunt*; *vertunt crateras aenos*; *concurrunt undique telis*; *tollitur in caelum clamor*; and many more, including the recurrent *divum pater atque hominum rex* and the description of Fabius in the prophetic speech of Anchises in the sixth book as *unus qui nobis cunctando restituis rem*. Sometimes a phrase thus echoed from Ennius is recognizable as a translation of a Homeric formula; for instance *sonitum super arma dedere* = ᾿αράβησε δὲ τεύχε᾿ ἐπ᾿ αὐτῷ, and very many other echoes of Homeric phrases can be felt throughout the Aeneid, in Latin versions which are no doubt sometimes Ennian and sometimes Virgil's own: *miseris mortalibus* =δειλοῖσι βροτοῖσι; *saevo pectore* = νηλέϊ θυμῷ; *lacrimabile bellum* = πόλεμον δακρυόεντα; *animo gratissime nostro* = ᾿εμῷ κεχαρισμένε θυμῷ; *sic fatur lacrimans* =ὣς φάτο δάκρυ χέων; *longe gradientem* = μακρὰ βιβάντα; *ensesque decoros* = φάσγανα καλά, to cite only a few random specimens of a very extensive category. These epic formulae are inherited. Others are perhaps coined on the model of them: *altae moenia Romae, Troiae sub moenibus altis, solio . . . ab alto* and the like. Certain homely processes, such as making fire or preparing a simple meal, are elaborately paraphrased, presumably to free them from associations felt to be too prosaic.[1]

Another way in which Virgil's diction departs from that of prose is in its syntax, in the way in which words are put together grammatically in the sentence. Sometimes, for instance, an adjective whose meaning relates primarily to one noun is attached grammatically to another (*recentem caede locum, purpurei cristis iuvenes, clara dedit sonitum tuba*),[2] or two nouns related by a verb have their normal relationship inverted (*excussa magistro navis, adlabi classibus aequor, neque me sententia vertit*).[3] Sometimes a phrase is compressed by omitting a term of meaning and leaving it to be supplied in thought: *excedere palma* (withdraw from *the contest for* the prize), *falsa sub proditione* (on a false *charge of* treachery), *timuit . . . pennis* (fluttered in alarm), *caeso sanguine* (blood *of* slaughtered *victims*);[4] and sometimes grammar as well as meaning needs to be completed by the imagination in this way: *quos dives Anagnia pascit, quos, Amasene pater* (sc. *tu pascis*); *non vitae gaudia quaero, sed nato Manes perferre sub imos* (sc. *gaudia*); *Aeneas equitum levia . . . arma praemisit, quaterent campos* (i.e. *ut* or *imperavitque ut quaterent. . . .*)[5] It will be seen that this flexibility of structure not only give variety to the diction, but also renders it more compact. Another element in it is a widening of the range of values to be got from the unassisted cases of the noun: from the genitive, for instance, in *urbis opus* (*big as* a city), *utero luporum* (Scylla's belly *sprouting* wolves), *aeris campis* (the *airy* plain), *ira deorum* (anger *against* the gods), *nati vulnera* (the wounds *dealt by* her son);[6] from the ablative in *clamore* (*with* loud cries), *gemitu* (*with* a groan), *flumine* (*by* the river), *talibus dictis* (*fired by* these words), *fuso crateres olivo* (bowls *filled with* oil), *domus sanie dapibusque cruentis* (the den *spattered with* gore from his cannibal meals).[7] Words whose function is purely syntactical tend to be omitted when the meaning can be obtained without them.

But more specifically Virgilian than the poetic colouring of the vocabulary and the poetic freedom of the syntax of the *Aeneid* is the coining of expressive original phrases out of extremely elementary words. Thus of a man struggling with an armed assailant is said *vim viribus exit* (struggling, he eludes the other's effort); Evander leads Aeneas into his modest dwelling with the words *rebusque veni non asper egenis* (do not scorn the welcome of a poor man's home); Aeneas has heard of Dido that she is no more and has *ferro . . . extrema secutam* (has sought an end with the sword); Turnus as signs of disaster crowd upon him is for a moment dazed, *varia confusus imagine rerum* (bewildered, his thoughts in a turmoil); as Aeneas sees the tale of Troy depicted on the temple-doors at Carthage he reflects *quae regio in terris nostri non plena laboris?* (is there any land in all the world that is not full of the tale of our suffering?); Latinus warns Turnus *respice res bello varias* (think of the changing fortunes of war); these are only random examples of a ubiquitous quality of style.[8] It extracts a variety of values, in combination, from basic or other simple verbs such as *do, fero, habeo, sequor, premo, tempto, tango, voco, misceo*; and from simple adjectives such as *durus, carus, caecus, fessus, ingens, vastus, mollis, asper, cavus, miser, aeger, varius*; and from simple nouns such as *res, vis, laus, mens, sors, labor, amor, finis, moles, honos, fortuna, imago*. Thus the anxious Trojans are urged by Anchises to consult Apollo and enquire *quam fessis finem rebus ferat, unde laborum temptare auxilium iubeat . . .*; and the disheartened Trojan women are torn, in Sicily, *miserum inter amorem praesentis terrae fatisque vocantia regna*.[9] One benefit of this method is a flexibility of diction which favours the creation of the Virgilian sound-patterns, of which more will be said below. Another is a kind of ambiguity which makes many Virgilian phrases capable of a variety of meanings additional to that determined by their immediate context in the poem. For instance, the sentence *quae regio in terris nostri non plena laboris?* means in its context 'what land is not full of the fame of our sufferings?', but in another context could mean 'what land is not full of the achievements of our people?', or 'is there a land in which our people have not toiled and suffered?'; and other shades of meaning are possible besides these. This is one of the reasons why so many of Virgil's phrases have seemed to later readers exactly apposite to contexts in their own experience quite different from those for which the poet framed them.

While some Virgilian phrases thus embrace many meanings, others are very precisely expressive of a single specific quality in a situation. This is sometimes achieved by the use of a word which is itself distinctive in form and meaning, but sometimes also by causing a common word to acquire a distinctive value from its context. In the former class come the many words of emotive value with the characteristic termination *-abilis*: *lamentabilis, inlaetabilis, ineluctabilis, immedicabilis, irreparabilis, inextricabilis, implacabilis, miserabilis, lacrimabilis, inamabilis* and the rest. In these the obviously emotive content of the word is reinforced by the distinctive form. Similarly in descriptive words such as *imperterritus, picturatas, increbrescere, desolavimus, circumfundimur, circumvolat, discriminat, remurmurat, subremigat* the descriptive effect is reinforced by the impact of the word's unusual length. The same is true with words of distinctive termination such as the adjectives in *-osus* (*villosus* = 'shaggy', *latebrosus* = 'full of crannies', *fragosus* = 'loud-roaring') and in *-ax* (*tenaci forcipe* = the tongs' grip, *nidis loquacibus* = the chirruping chicks in the nest, *ignis edax* = the devouring flames). And it is true also, and in a higher degree, with the verbs that have the frequentative terminations *-so* and *-to* (*rapto, volito, prenso, pulso, lapso*, etc.), or the inceptive termination *-esco* (*inardesco, ignesco, claresco, silesco, languesco, tremesco*, etc.). In most of these the distinctive form of the word stimulates the attention and at the same time the process that it brings to mind is one that stirs a positive and specific response of recognition: thus *lapso* describes the repeated skidding of the feet in a slippery area, *prenso* the clawing of hands that strive unsuccessfully to get a grip, *recepto* the tugging effort to free something that is stuck; similarly *albesco* is said of the gradual lightening of the sky at daybreak, *claresco* of sound becoming louder and more identifiable as it draws nearer, *liquesco* of a solid beginning to melt.[10] These all evoke exactly an experience or observation that is at once recognized, and *felt* in the process of recognition. And this distinctiveness of meaning is matched by a corresponding distinctiveness of form.

On the other hand an equally exact expressiveness is often achieved by the co-operation of a context with a common word which is in itself of wide and general application and so stirs, unaided, no particular response. The banqueters in Dido's palace *vocem . . . per ampla volutant atria*; and here the context, the swelling and rolling noise of the festivities (itself conveyed by the rather distinctive word *volutant*) makes the familiar adjective *ampla* strongly significant of the spaciousness of the hall and the corridors and other apartments through which the echoes sound.[11] Similarly when Polites pursued by Pyrrhus *porticibus longis fugit et vacua atria lustrat* the familiar adjectives *longis* and *vacua* identify emotive features in the special situation and become strongly significant themselves in so doing; they lead the imagination to supply the suspense of the onlookers, the echoing footsteps of the runners and so on.[12] A still clearer example is in the description of the sea-nymph Cymodoce as she holds the stern of Aeneas' ship with one hand while she paddles with the other beneath the surface: *et laeva tacitis subremigat undis*. Here the familiar word *tacitis* draws attention to a very distinctive phenomenon which stirs a quick response in the reader and brings the moment alive for him, the curious soundlessness of motion seen through water.[13] In all these cases and many others like them the common word identifies a distinctive feature in the context, and the context thus extracts from the common word a particular and valuable meaning. The working of the process can be studied further in the variety of effects obtained by the poet from the familiar adjectives *ingens* and *cavus*. From *ingens*, which indicates size with connotations of mass, come *ingens argentum* (massive silverware), *ingentem fumum* (the huge cloud of dense smoke belched out by the fire-breathing giant), *ingens clamor* (the tremendous shout of an army), *iussis ingentibus* (the stern and insistent commands of an oracular god), *ingenti mole* (the ponderous mass of a stricken warrior as he crashes to the ground), *ingenti . . . umbra* (the huge and menacing shadow of a warrior seen looming by his fallen foe).[14] From *cavus*, which indicates hollowness and can suggest various implications attaching to this concept, come *cavae plangoribus aedes femineis ululant* (the palace *echoes* with their cries), *multa cavo lateri ingeminant* (the boxers deal *thudding body-blows*), *manibus . . . lacessunt pectora plausa cavis* (the grooms *pat* and *slap* the horses as they work on them), *cava tempora ferro traicit* (Ascanius' arrow goes through the man's temples as through a *fragile shell*), *cava sub imagine formae* (the ghosts are *empty shapes*), *nox atra cava circumvolat umbra* (the darkness *seems to envelop* him and flap and flutter about him).[15] A similar diversity of emotive values, in varying degrees, is extracted by different contexts from other common adjectives, such as *mollis, durus, asper, aeger, caecus, vastus, clarus, varius, incertus,* and many more.

All said so far has been about the element of poetry that resides in the meanings and connotations of words. Another element resides in the rhythm and sounds which they make in combination. This element makes its own independent appeal to the ear of the reader, but also co-operates in various ways with the meaning that is being at the same time communicated to his mind. In the management of it the poet has three kinds of resource at his disposal.

First of these of course is the regular rhythm imposed throughout on the poet's statement by the hexameter metre. This rhythm, fixed though it is, admits continually two sorts of internal variation. On the one hand, every one of the six feet that make up the hexameter line (except the last) may be either a dactyl with the value – ∪ ∪ or a spondee with the value – –, subject to the provision that there will always be at least one dactyl in the line; with the result that some twenty different combinations of dactyls and spondees are possible and provide a continual variety of pattern.[16] On the other hand, in every foot there may also be either coincidence or non-coincidence of the beat suggested by the movement of the verse with the accent placed on the words by ordinary pronunciation: thus in *spargens umida mella soporiferumque papaver* there is coincidence of speech-accent and verse-beat in every foot of the line, whereas in *dat latus: insequitur cumulo praeruptus aquae mons* there is coincidence in none; and again a wide variety of patterns is available between these two exceptional extremes.[17] The metrical system thus combines strict regularity in one respect with elaborate variety in others.

Secondly, the whole range of artifices by which the prose-writer, and the orator especially, imposes form and pattern on his discourse are available also to the poet. These include the familiar figures of sentence-structure such as chiasmus (reversal of word-order in successive phrases, as in *spem vultu simulat, premit altum corde dolorem*), and anaphora (repetition of a word at the beginning of successive phrases, as in *iam matura viro, iam plenis nubilis annis*), and juxtaposition of the same word in different cases (*illum absens absentem auditque videtque*), and many others; but above all the adjustment of the lengths of the various members of a sentence or paragraph to assist a rhythmical delivery of it in pronunciation. It is a characteristic of Virgil's management of the hexameter that he has freed the evolution of his sentence and paragraph-structure from excessive servitude to the uniformly recurrent pauses suggested by the regularity of the metre. An example such as

> Aeolus haec contra: 'Tuus, o regina, quid optes
> explorare labor; mihi iussa capessere fas est.
> tu mihi quodcumque hoc regni, tu sceptra Iovemque
> concilias, tu das epulis accumbere divum
> nimborumque facis tempestatumque potentem.'   (l. 76–80)

is typical of the way in which he weaves a rhetorically-contrived pattern of sentence structure over the metrical pattern of the verse.

Thirdly, there is the patterning of the sound of the whole by assonance, as in

> desine meque tuis incendere teque querelis   (4.360)

and alliteration, as in

> at regina gravi iamdudum saucia cura
> vulnus alit venis et caeco carpitur igni.
> multa viri virtus animo multusque recursat
> gentis honos: haerent infixi pectore vultus
> verbaque, nec placidam membris dat cura quietem.   (4.1–5)

This kind of patterning of the sound is present everywhere in various forms and in varying degree, but it becomes more insistent in emotionally important passages. It is necessary to be aware of its presence and sensitive to its effect, because Latin poets, and Latin prose-writers also, paid great attention to the *sound* of their style, being led to this, as Quintilian says, by the consciousness that Latin was a less naturally euphonious language than Greek and that the deficiency had to be supplied by the art of the writer.* This does not mean of course that the writer thinks or works in terms of the letters of the alphabet and their possible combinations, but that his ear seeks a

---

* Quintilian, 12.10.27–36. While for this reason Latin education laid a particular emphasis on the element of sound in style, sensitivity to this was general in a world in which the normal way of reading to oneself was to read aloud; thus Philip, in *Acts* 8.26 ff., could *hear* the eunuch of the Ethiopian queen reading Isaiah to himself when he approached his chariot on the road from Jerusalem to Gaza.

certain quality of sound in a given context. This sound is yielded by
certain combinations of the values represented by letters, and these
can be observed in print. But what the writer is aware of is the
sound he wants, not its alphabetical foundations.

The rhythms produced by metre and sentence-structure, and the
sounds produced by alliteration and assonance afford a certain
pleasure in their own right. But they also can serve in various ways
to assist the meaning or the feeling that the poet is trying to
communicate.

For instance, the movement of a line will be fast or slow according
as dactyls or spondees predominate in it. And obviously a faster
movement is appropriate to some subjects and a slower movement
to others. Thus in

> illi inter sese multa vi bracchia iactant   (8.452)

or

> centum aerei claudunt vectes aeternaque ferri
> robora . . .   (7.609–10)

or

> infelix! nati funus crudele videbis   (11.53)

the slow movement of the line is appropriate to the effort with which
the smiths heave up in turn their heavy hammers, and to the
massive solidity of the barred and bolted door, and to the thought
of the bereaved father's heavy loss. On the other hand, in

> illa pharetram
> fert umero, gradiensque deas supereminet omnis   (1.500–1)

and

> ipse manu magna Portunus euntem
> impulit: illa noto citius volucrique sagitta   (5.241–3)
> ad terram fugit . . .

and

> quadrupedante putrem sonitu quatit ungula campum   (8.596)

the quick dactylic movement suits the swift stride of the goddess, and
the spurt which shoots the vessel through the water, and the brisk
action of the horses.

Again, the rhythms of rhetoric—the kind of rhythms exemplified
in St. Paul's chapter on Charity, or Lincoln's speech at Gettysburg—

LANGUAGE AND SENSIBILITY   69

have obviously the power to enhance the emotive effect of a statement.[18] This effect will be felt in Virgil not only in speeches, such as the perorations of Jupiter in the first book and of Anchises in the sixth, but in narrative and descriptive passages as well—for instance, in the description of Camilla which comes in the seventh book at the end of the catalogue of assembling Italian forces.

Lastly, the sound value of the syllables composing a sentence can reinforce its meaning in more ways than one. Thus in the line quoted above

> centum aerei claudunt vectes aeternaque ferri
> robora

the preponderance of heavy double consonants and diphthongs makes heavy as well as slow this description of the ponderous door. Likewise in the line

> quadrupedante putrem sonitu quatit ungula campum

the quality of the double consonants accords with the emphatic beat of the horses' hooves, and differentiates the effect of the line in this respect from that of the equally dactylic line describing the swift spurt of the ship: both motions are fast, but the ship's is a very different type of motion from that of the horse.

Another example of the relevance of sound to sense is afforded by Dido's curse

> exoriare aliquis nostris ex ossibus ultor   (4.625)

in which the alliterations on *r* and *s* invite pronunciation as a growl and hiss. And this is instructive; for in the description of the Sleep-god tempting Palinurus

> pone caput fessosque oculos furare labori:
> ipse ego paulisper pro te tua munera inibo   (5.845–6)

the alliteration on the same letters corresponds to a murmur and a whisper. It needs therefore to be emphasized that the effect of the sound-value of the words in such cases is not (unless very rarely) to *convey* sense, but to reinforce it with a suitable accompaniment. This obviously occurs most easily when a sound of some kind is an important element in the context, as is the tone of voice of the speaker in the two passages just cited. The point is illustrated further in many of Virgil's descriptions: the galloping horses

> gemit ultima pulsu
> Thraca pedum, circumque atrae formidinis ora

and the blaring trumpet of Misenus

> quo non praest*ant*ior *alt*er
> aere ciere viros, Mar*tem*que ac*cend*ere *cant*u   (6.164–5)

and the succession of rolling thunder-claps

> iterum atque iterum fragor increpat ingens   (8.527)

and the ship striking a submerged rock

> con*c*ussae *c*autes, et a*c*uto muri*c*e remi
> obni*x*ae *c*repuere   (5.205–6)

In all of these the subject being described involves a distinctive
sound, with which the sound made by the words can be felt to
harmonize.

But sometimes the case is not so simple. There are many passages
in which what is being described is soundless, and yet a sound-
pattern in the wording can be felt to assist the effect of the description. Take for example Virgil's picture of a shooting star

> de caelo lapsa per *um*bram
> stella fa*c*em d*uc*ens multa *cum* lu*c*e *cuc*urrit   (2.693–4)

or of the morning star rising from the sea

> qualis ubi *O*ceani perf*us*us L*u*cifer *u*nda,
> quem Venus ante ali*os* astrorum d*i*lig*it* *i*gnis,
> extul̦it *os* sacrum cael*o* tenebrasque resolvit   (8.589–91)

or of the rising of the brilliant and baneful dog-star

> S*ir*ius ard*or*
> *ill*e s*it*im m*or*bosque ferens m*or*talibus *ae*gris
> nascitur et *lae*vo contristat *lu*mine c*ae*lum   (10.273–5)

or the miraculous flame that envelopes Lavinia as she stands by her
father's side at the sacrifice

> tum f*um*ida l*um*ine f*ulv*o
> in*volv*i, et totis *Volc*anum spargere tectis   (7.76–7)

In all of these the scene described is one in which light, not sound,
is the principal ingredient; yet in each, surely, the sound of the
passage can be felt to enhance its effect, which is meant to be felt as
remarkable because the context is important—a miraculous occurrence, or a simile introduced to illustrate and emphasize an important moment in the story. What seems to happen is that the

reader's ear is aware in these passages of certain sound-patterns which are both distinctive and unusual, and his sensibility to the meaning of the passage is stimulated thereby. It is perhaps worth remarking too that the sounds repeated in forming the sound pattern often include the dominant sound in a word whose meaning is important: that, for instance, in the stressed syllable of *luce*, and so too in *ignis*, and *os*, and *Sirius*, and *morbos*, and *aegris*, and *lumine* and *involvi*. But whatever the explanation of the working of the effect, the fact and the value of it are hardly in doubt.

The poet's command of expressive words and his ability to reinforce this expressiveness by the sounds he makes with them co-operates with, and is indeed inseparably involved with, an awareness of details of common experience which though common are not commonplace, and which by being common enable him to speak through them to the common reader, and by being not common-place excite in the reader a quick and interested response. This response may be one of immediate recognition, or of realization of something now perceived as true but not before apprehended; and which it is, depends of course on the individual reader. For instance, the *monochrome* of twilight, in which things have shape but not colour, was a simple fact that I had not myself apprehended until it was pointed out to me by Virgil's comparison of the gloom of the under-world to a dim moonlight in which *rebus nox abstulit atra colorem*, but to others the realization must have come as no surprise.[19] On the other hand, when Virgil speaks of shooting stars 'detaching themselves' from the sky, I recognize at once the curious and distinctive effect that he is describing; and so too when he speaks of lightning as a 'gleaming crack running across the dark clouds' I recognize at once the equally distinctive appearance of one kind of lightning as a brilliant flickering filament on the horizon with the irregular contour of a crack in a piece of china.[20]

This kind of observation is ubiquitous. Sea-side scenes provide a number of examples: the effect of a shower of hail falling into the sea; a storm-cloud as it approaches rapidly over the sea, cutting off the sunlight and preceded by a squall of wind; a mass of stone and concrete let down into the sea in some process of construction-work, as it topples, sinks and slowly settles on the bottom, and the sea swirls and surges, and a cloud of sand rises in the water around it; a rock is beaten by the waves and the seaweed is slapped against it and slithers back into the water; a wave runs up on to the shore and covers the rocks, frothing, and spreads in a curve over the beach, and then runs back dragging the pebbles with it as it retires.[21] These instances are as it happens all from similes, but others can be drawn in abundance from the narrative itself; from fire-scenes for instance: the collapse of the crust of ash and the dying of the flames as a fire burns itself out; the way in which embers soak up liquid poured on them; the warmth of the soil which has been heaped on the remnants of a fire; the dust-laden smoke of a conflagration heaving and bellying in a confined space, and the ash and cinders from a conflagration eddying far off in the air.[22] The facts observed here are all recognizable from anyone's experience, and thus speak to everyone. They are also distinctive and evocative in a way that stimulates the reader's response and so makes real to him the context in which they are recalled.

A series of evocative touches of this kind may be combined in a descriptive tableau, such as that of the voyage in the third book or the fall of Troy in the second. In the story of the voyage any reader will recognize, consciously or sub-consciously, the impressions of land seen from an approaching or receding vessel, of the contrasting varieties of island scenery and the changing features of a coastal landscape, of the noise of breakers on reefs in the distance, and echoes from cliffs near at hand, and mysterious sounds coming across the water from an unidentified origin on the shore. Equally recognizable from common experience (even if from very different contexts) are many components of the story of the last night of Troy: the menace of ominous sounds coming nearer and growing louder, the reflection of fire in the sea, human figures looming up suddenly through the half-light, the sound of a man's own voice in the darkness and solitude as he calls the name of the companion who does not answer—these are only a few examples from a much larger number that might be adduced. In other contexts, again, an essential quality in a general situation may be conveyed by no more than one or two significant particulars that touch on universal but distinctive experience in the same way. The contrast between the living Aeneas, a creature of flesh and blood, and the unsubstantial ghosts in the underworld is made real by the creaking and leaking of Charon's boat as he steps into it, and by the faint sounds that issue from the mouths of the indignant ghosts when they try to shout aloud.[23] The rural peace of the setting of Aeneas' visit to Evander is expressed in the silent gliding of his ship among the trees and the bird-song that wakes him on the following morning.[24] The public consequences of Dido's absorption in her love are illustrated with a vignette of suspended work and unfinished constructions at Carthage, with the huge cranes, idle, at the centre of it.[25] Similar touches may intensify the reality of a tragic moment; as the great groan rises from the watching army when Turnus falls in the final duel, or as Priam slips and lurches in the blood on the floor while Pyrrhus drags him to his death.[26]

The reader of the *Aeneid* soon discovers that Virgil speaks to him not only through the shared responsiveness to things seen and heard with which much of the discussion above has been concerned, but also through a sympathetic awareness of inward experiences: craving, temptation, self-conflict, remorse, fatigue, defeat, bereavement, fear for loved ones, the dawning realization of error or moral failing, and much else. It would not be profitable to attempt a detailed illustration here of the ways in which this awareness displays itself in the story, but one aspect of it has a particular relevance to the present chapter. In both Dido and Turnus an inward crisis already impending is precipitated by the special impact of an external event vividly presented; in Dido by sight of the empty harbour in the dawn, in Turnus by the burst of flame from the tower on the walls of the city whose defender he has set himself to be.[27]

This chapter has been concerned with the efficacy of Virgil's poetry as a medium simply for the telling of his story. But a passing mention was made above of a certain widely evocative quality in many Virgilian phrases which has made later readers feel them apt to contexts in their own experience quite other than those in which they occur in Virgil's poem. R. A. Knox makes a character in one of his books observe that 'Virgil has the gift . . . of summing up in a phrase used at random the tragedy and the aspiration of minds that he could never have understood'; and the same thought was illustrated, almost a century ago, in some pages of F. W. H. Myers' once-celebrated essay.[28] This evocative quality attaches not only to Virgil's language but also to many motifs and incidents in the story of the *Aeneid*, which have acquired thereby a significance for later ages which the poet cannot have foreseen but which have become a now inseparable part of his poem's effect. The story of men who left their homes to make a new home beyond the sea, of the fusion of races and cultures in a people's past, of the birth of greatness out of disaster has its evident analogies in the histories of other nations. The vocation of Aeneas has its analogy in other vocations, religious or secular, of individual human beings. Motifs such as the call, the journey, the promised land, the hope of a city, the vision of the future vouchsafed, the descent into the darkness, the crossing of the river—these evoke a whole set of corresponding motifs in post-Virgilian tradition, and evoke with them the symbolic significances that these have acquired. And there are other things in the *Aeneid*, such as the golden bough and the ivory door, which are not less suggestive because their import remains mysterious, like the magic casements in Keats' sonnet.

The language and story of the *Aeneid* are evocative also in another way, through the echoes which pervade it of past literature and of past and contemporary events in Roman history. The nature of this resonance will be illustrated in the course of the chapters now about to follow.

MAKING THE STORY: FUSION OF THE LEGEND OF AENEAS' COMING TO ITALY WITH MATTER FROM ILIAD AND ODYSSEY

THE *Aeneid* is a poem wholly different in character from the Homeric poems. Yet it recalls them on every page, and is constructed largely by the re-moulding of Homeric materials. The extent and nature of this process can best be appreciated if we compare the contributions to the substance of the poem made respectively by the legend of the coming of Aeneas to Italy and by the Homeric Iliad and Odyssey, in which Aeneas plays no very considerable part.

A prose version of the legend of Aeneas' journey from Troy to Latium, and of his settlement there and marriage with the Latin princess Lavinia and warfare with the neighbouring inhabitants, is available to us in the *Roman Antiquities* (1.49–53 and 55–60 with 64–5) of the Greek historian Dionysius of Halicarnassus, who wrote at Rome in the Augustan age. As regards the journey this is the only consecutive account that we have for comparison with Virgil's. As regards the arrival in Italy and subsequent warfare we have also the account of Livy (1.1–3), and brief and not always coherent summaries in the Servian commentary on the *Aeneid* (on *Aeneid* 1.259, 1.267, 4.620, 6.760, 9.742, 11.316),[1] and in Strabo's *Geography* (5.3.2) and elsewhere. These suffice to show the outline of the story current in Virgil's day and the relation of the story he tells in the *Aeneid* to this.

The course of the Trojans' travels as given by Dionysius is as follows. From Troy they go first to Aeneia in Thrace; thence to Delos in the Cyclades, where Anius is king; thence to the island of Cythera, off the south of the Peloponnese; thence, after touching at a promontory of the Peloponnese, to Zacynthus in the Ionian islands (where they institute a sacrifice and games, said by Dionysius to be still held in his own time); thence to Leucas, Actium, Ambracia, Buthrotum on the west coast of Epirus (whence Aeneas visits the Trojan Helenus and the oracle of Dodona, some way inland); thence to Onchesmus a little further up the coast, and from Onchesmus across the strait to Italy, where some land at the Sallentine pro-

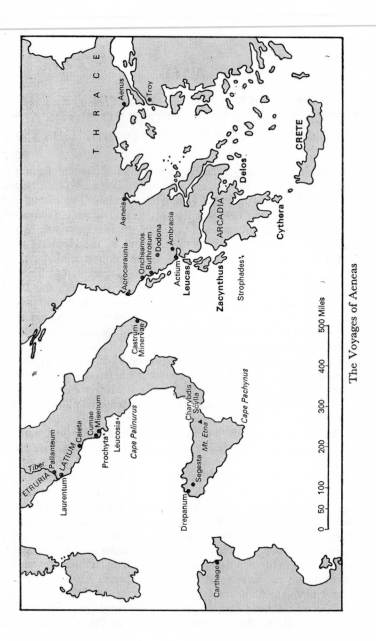

The Voyages of Aeneas

THRACE

Aenus
Troy

Aeneia
Acroceraunia
Onchesmos
Buthrotum
Dodona
Ambracia
Actium
Leucas
Zacynthus
Strophades
ARCADIA
Delos
Cythera
CRETE

Castrum
Minervae

Tiber
Pallanteum
ETRURIA
LATIUM
Laurentum
Caieta
Cumae
Misenum
Prochyta
Leucosia
Cape Palinurus

Charybdis
Scylla
Drepanum
Segesta
Mt. Etna
Cape Pachynus

Carthage

0   50 100   200   300   400   500 Miles

montory at the tip of the heel of Italy and some a little to the north
at Castrum Minervae; thence around the south coast of Italy to the
straits of Messina (identified by the ancients with the location of the
Homeric Scylla and Charybdis); thence ('perhaps because forced off
their course by a storm') they arrive at Drepanum in the north-*west*
corner of Sicily, where they find earlier Trojan colonists established
and help to found the city of Segesta (to settle some of their number
who are travel-weary, or 'as others say' because a number of their
ships have been destroyed by mutinous women); thence they cross
the Tyrrhenian sea and land at Cape Palinurus on the west coast of
Italy, and proceed up the coast via Leucosia, Misenum, Prochyta,
Caieta (at all of which members of the company die, giving their
names to these places) to Laurentum near the Tiber estuary, 'where
they made an entrenched camp . . . distant about four stades from
the sea'.

It is clear that Virgil starts from the same basic account as
Dionysius, for he makes Aeneas follow in outline the same decidedly
complicated route: Troy—Thrace—southward to Delos—around
the south of the Peloponnese to Epirus—across the straits of Otranto
to south-east Italy—around the foot of Italy to the straits of Messina
—thence to north-west Sicily—across the Tyrrhenian sea to the west
coast of Italy—up the west coast to the Tiber estuary. Naturally
enough he has cut out a number of halts in the interests of simplicity
and concentration: on the coast of Peloponnese for instance, and at
Ambracia, and at Cape Palinurus and Leucosia and Prochyta. But
also he has introduced variations. He takes Aeneas not to Cythera
but to Crete; and not to Zacynthus but to some small islands (the
Strophades) to the south of it where the legendary Harpies, in his
account, have made their home. For the visit to Crete he had no
doubt authority, as it were, in the existence of a town in Crete
called Pergamum which was by some supposed to be a Trojan
colony. But the visit to the Harpies' islands is obviously contrived in
order to enable Aeneas to share an experience with Jason and the
Argonauts, just as he later lands near the abode of the Cyclops to
share an experience with Ulysses, and it shows that Virgil is prepared
to use his invention in modifying the account from which he starts
in order to suit his own purposes. It was convenient to keep Aeneas
away from Cythera and Zacynthus because this avoided the com-
plications of an encounter with presumably hostile Greeks. It was
expedient to bring him to the Harpies' islands for the reason already
stated, and to Crete for the sake of the story of the misunderstood

oracle which illustrates the initial uncertainty of the Trojans about where they are going.[2] But a much more important variation than either of these is that which brings Aeneas to Carthage and not only introduces the story of Dido's tragic love and death but also determines the structural design of the whole of the first third of the poem. The basic account exhibited by Dionysius does not bring Aeneas to Carthage at all; and the fact that the visit to Carthage has been superimposed on the basic account is to be seen from the way in which it is attached: the Trojans have left Drepanum in north-west Sicily on their way to their final destination when they are carried to Carthage by the storm with which the poem opens, and when they leave Carthage at the end of the fourth book they return to Drepanum again, so that the whole event is a digression. Whether in making this crucial modification of the basic account which he shares with Dionysius Virgil is simply inventing or is eclectically intruding an item from another account we cannot be sure; nor does it matter much. It is usually supposed that Naevius in his *Bellum Punicum* had brought Aeneas to Carthage; but this is uncertain.[3]

Concerning events in Italy after the Trojans reach the end of their journey, the accounts of Dionysius, Strabo and Livy agree broadly, despite variations of detail, with the outline given by the expanded version of the Servian commentary on *Aeneid* 1.259. According to this account (for which no authority is named) Aeneas is accepted as an ally by King Latinus at their first encounter and given the princess Lavinia as his bride; the Rutulian prince Turnus, who had hoped to marry her himself, then makes war on Latinus and Aeneas; in the ensuing battle Latinus and Turnus are killed and Aeneas disappears; a further war follows between Mezentius, king of the Etruscans and ally of Turnus, and Aeneas' son Ascanius. Livy in giving a corresponding account mentions also a variant version of the beginning of the story, according to which there is first a battle between the Trojans and Latins in which the Trojans are victorious, and it is only after this that Latinus allies himself with Aeneas and gives him Lavinia for wife and the other events follow as above described.

These broadly synoptic versions of the story obviously differ in important respects from the version given in the *Aeneid*. One major point of difference is that in the synoptic version of the prose authors the Latins and Trojans are allied in resistance to Turnus, whereas in Virgil the Latins (despite the reluctance of King Latinus) are allied with Turnus against the Trojans. Virgil's version may here reflect an account (perhaps one of alternatives) given by Cato a century and a half before; for the Servian notes on *Aeneid* 1.267 and 4.620 speak, or seem to speak of Cato as recording that depredations committed by the Trojans led to fighting 'against Latinus and Turnus' in which Latinus was killed and Turnus routed. But it is possible that these notes merely give a garbled version of the alternative recorded by Livy (see above) in which the Trojans *first* fight a battle against Latinus and then *later* a battle (in alliance now with Latinus) against Turnus; for many Servian notes certainly are garbled, and the Servian note on *Aeneid* 6.760 attributes to Cato a version similar to the 'synoptic' one. It is an open question whether in this matter Virgil's divergence from the synoptic version is due to eclecticism or to free invention. In other matters it is clear that he has given his invention very free rein. For instance, in all the other accounts there is a series of wars spread over some length of time: Virgil has telescoped these into a single affair lasting only a few days. In all the other accounts Latinus is killed in battle early in the war: Virgil makes him survive it, and indeed take no part in the fighting. In all the other accounts the Etruscan king Mezentius survives Aeneas and engages after Aeneas' death in warfare with his son Ascanius: Virgil makes him fall by Aeneas' hand. In no other account are the Etruscan people at enmity with their king: this is a prominent feature of Virgil's story. Finally, in no other account do the Arcadians and Evander and Pallas figure at all; in the *Aeneid* the visit of Aeneas to Pallanteum and the death of Pallas at Turnus' hands are not only prominent features of the story but major factors determining its structure, producing the divided action of Books 8–9 and the theme of the quest for vengeance in Books 10–12.

It will be seen from this that Virgil has very drastically departed from the version of the legend which seems to have been commonly current in his day, and that his own version in the *Aeneid* has been produced partly perhaps by eclectic adoption of elements from earlier variants, of which no doubt there were many, but also (it would appear) by freely recasting the current version to suit his own creative purpose. It will be noticed further that the most important variation both in the story of the wanderings and in the story of the war has been achieved by amalgamating with the Aeneas legend a legend properly distinct from it. For Dido had her own legend (see note 12 on p. 149), in which Aeneas played no part, but she killed herself to escape being forced to accept marriage with one of the

African princes, because she could not endure to break her vow of
fidelity to the memory of her dead husband Sychaeus. And Evander
had his own legend, in which Aeneas played no part, as founder of
the Arcadian settlement on the site of future Rome and host of
Hercules on his way back to Greece with the cattle of Geryon, when
Hercules killed the monster Cacus (Dionysius, 1.31–33 and 40,
Livy 1.7.4–15, Strabo 5.3.3). In bringing the Dido-legend and the
Evander-legend into the story of Aeneas—whether with precedent
or without—Virgil has provided the two elements which dominate
the structure of the two halves of his story. It is a curious fact too that
in both cases there is associated with the process a motif suggested
by the *Argonautica* of Apollonius Rhodius. For the sudden and con-
suming love of Dido for Aeneas very evidently contains a reflection
of the sudden love of Medea for Jason in the *Argonautica*; and in the
person of Pallas, the old king's young son who is sent by his father
to accompany the hero when he goes on his way, there is a reflection, faint but unmistakable, of Daskylus the son of Lycus the king
of the Mariandyni who is sent by his father to accompany Jason.[4]
Also associated with the introduction of the Dido-legend and the
Evander-legend is, in each case, a reminiscence of Homer, and it is
these reminiscences which shape the structure of the poem as a
whole. For the Carthaginian episode serves like the Phaeacian
episode of the *Odyssey* as setting of the hero's retrospective narrative
of his past adventures, and like that episode of the *Odyssey* it is
brought into the story by a storm. This provides the structural
coherence of Books 1–4. Similarly the visit of Aeneas to Pallanteum
makes the occasion of the attack on the Trojan camp in his absence,
and creates the divided action in the first part of the war story which
parallels in miniature the divided action of the first two-thirds of the
Iliad; while the death of Pallas at the hand of Turnus and Aeneas'
quest for vengeance, finally achieved, on the slayer of his friend
provide the theme which gives coherence to the latter part of the war
story in *Aeneid* 10–12. It is thus from Homer that Virgil has drawn
the ideas that shape the outline of his version of the Aeneas-legend;
and in applying them he has drawn material from the Dido-legend
and the Evander-legend, and from Apollonius' version of the Jason-
legend too.

The contribution of Homer to the fabric of the *Aeneid* is not of
course confined to the ideas which shape its outline as described
above. A high proportion of the events which develop the story or
occur as episodes in the course of it have been suggested by remini-

scence of the *Iliad* or the *Odyssey*. Thus, the sequence of detailed events that run from the storm with which the action of the poem begins to Aeneas' first conversation with Dido in the first book is largely made up of sporadic echoes of events in *Odyssey* 5–13. In narrating his past adventures to his hosts in Books 2 and 3 Aeneas is of course following the example of Ulysses in *Odyssey* 9–12. The games held in honour of Anchises in book 5 are a counterpart of the games held for Patroclus in *Iliad* 23, and most of the individual items correspond as well as the general conception. The visit of Aeneas to the world of the dead in Book 6 corresponds in the same way to Ulysses' experience in *Odyssey* 11. The catalogue of the assembling Latin peoples in Book 7 corresponds to the catalogue of the Achaeans in *Iliad* 2. The scenes of the arrival of Aeneas at Pallanteum in Book 8 and of his early morning conversation with his host on the next day recall similar scenes at Pylos and Sparta in the travels of Telemachus in *Odyssey* 3 and 4. The gift of arms by Venus to her son at the end of the same Book 8 is counterpart of the gift of arms by Thetis to Achilles in *Iliad* 18. The night sortie of Nisus and Euryalus in Book 9 is counterpart of the night sortie of Ulysses and Diomede in *Iliad* 10. The fighting at the wall of the camp in the same Book 9 corresponds to the fighting at the wall of the Achaean camp in *Iliad* 12, and within it the act of Pandarus and Bitias in opening the gate to challenge the attackers recalls the similar act of Polypoetes and Leonteus in the *Iliad*. The beginning of a new phase of the action in Book 10 is marked by a Council of the Gods as in *Iliad* 8; and in the same book the catalogue of the relieving forces recalls the catalogue of the relieving Myrmidons in *Iliad* 16. The battle in Book 10 is opened by Aeneas in the same terms as by Agamemnon in *Iliad* 11; the feats and death of Pallas recall the feats and death of Patroclus in *Iliad* 16; the consequent rage of Aeneas and his furious progress recall the condition of Achilles in *Iliad* 20–1; and the phantom which deceives Turnus recalls (though its role is not the same) the phantom which deceives Achilles at the end of *Iliad* 21. In the following Book 11 the truce for the burial of the dead and the council in the enemies' camp correspond to the same events in *Iliad* 7; the interruption of the council by the approach of the Trojans corresponds to the interruption of the Trojans' council in *Iliad* 2 by the approach of the Achaeans; and the procession of the women to the citadel to pray for Athena's help corresponds to the procession and prayers of the women in *Iliad* 6. In Book 12 the truce for the duel and the breaking of the truce have been suggested by events in *Iliad* 3 and 4;

the temporary disablement of Aeneas recalls the temporary disablement of Hector in *Iliad* 14; and the final duel of Aeneas and Turnus
is counterpart of the duel between Achilles and Hector in *Iliad* 22.
This long list, though very far from exhaustive, will give an idea of
how much of the content of the *Aeneid* has been suggested by the
Homeric poems. This does not of course mean that Virgil is all the
time repeating Homer but that his invention finds much of its raw
material in reminiscence of the Homeric poems: the final product is
always distinctively his own. Nor is Homer the only literary ante-
cedent on which he draws in this way: Book 4 has little of Homer but
much of Dido's own story and of Apollonius' Medea: the fall of
Troy in Book 2 and the person of Camilla, the woman warrior in
Book 11, owe something presumably to the Epic Cycle but nothing
significant to the *Iliad* or the *Odyssey*.[5] But to a very large extent the
story told in the *Aeneid* is made by re-moulding Homeric materials,
as well as owing to Homer the broad motifs which govern its design.[6]
    By contrast the contribution of the Aeneas-legend itself to the
content of Virgil's story is, in substance, surprisingly limited. In
all the first half of the poem it has provided only the content of
Book 3 and of the two lines at the beginning and end of Book 6 which
record the landing of the Trojans at Cumae and Caieta; perhaps
also the firing of the ships by the rebellious women and the settlement of the travel-weary at Segesta in Book 5. In the story of events
in Latium, that is to say in the second half of the poem, the data
provided by the legend can be stated as follows: 'the king of the
Latins, Latinus, consents to allow the Trojans to settle and to
receive Aeneas as a friend, and is ready to give him his daughter
Lavinia in marriage. A neighbouring prince, the Rutulian Turnus,
who had hoped to marry Lavinia himself, makes war on the Trojans
and is assisted by the Etruscan king Mezentius. In the fighting
Turnus is killed.' All the substance in the second half of the *Aeneid*
which clothes this outline has been supplied by Virgil, and that not
only by the adaptation of Homeric motifs, but also by introducing
the Arcadians and the Etruscan people into the story as allies of the
Trojans, together with such striking episodes as the exploits and
death of Mezentius and the exploits and death of Camilla. Thus the
data of the legend have been both copiously supplemented and
freely modified in the making of the *Aeneid*.
    The freedom Virgil has used in modifying as well as supplement-
ing these data has been illustrated above with reference to major
features; it can be illustrated further with reference to details. Thus

Dionysius' version (D.H. 1.57) speaks of the 'family gods' appearing in a vision to Aeneas after his arrival in Latium, and this no doubt lies behind the apparition of the Penates (with a different message) in Crete in Book 3 of the *Aeneid*. Dionysius' version also speaks (D.H. 1.55) of a Sibyl on Mount Ida bidding the Trojans sail westward until they reach a land where they 'eat their tables', and this prophecy in the *Aeneid* is attributed in Book 3 to the Harpy Celaeno and in Book 7 to Anchises; as for the Sibyl of Ida, she has disappeared, to be replaced by a Cumaean Sibyl at a different stage of the story. Sometimes a variant mentioned by Dionysius can be recognized in the *Aeneid* in an even more remarkably altered dress. He records for instance (D.H. 1.72) an ancient tale that some of the *Greeks* homeward bound from Troy found themselves in Latium and wintered there, and were obliged to settle because Trojan women whom they had taken as captives set fire to their ships: this evidently lies behind the quite different account in the *Aeneid* of the end of the Trojans' ships after their arrival in Latium, perhaps also behind the burning of the ships by the Trojan women in Sicily. In such cases Virgil can be observed to be using motifs from the legend, as he often does motifs from previous poetry, to contribute to a new imaginative picture by a kind of kaleidoscopic rearrangement.

MAKING AN EPISODE: FUSION OF
INHERITED MATERIALS EXEMPLIFIED
IN THE SIXTH BOOK

THE last chapter illustrated the process by which Virgil throughout the *Aeneid* is adapting motifs from Homer to make his story, within the loose framework provided by the data (themselves adapted) of the Aeneas legend. The present chapter will attempt to illustrate, by reference to a single book, the process by which material from Homer is fused with material from a number of other observable sources in the making of a particular episode. The book chosen is the sixth. It is one of the most interesting books in the poem, and a study of it may also illustrate incidentally a number of other matters which have been discussed in earlier chapters.

The legend of Aeneas' coming to Italy, as we have seen, associates the names of a number of places on the west coast of Italy with the names of companions of Aeneas who were supposed to have died at them: Palinurus the pilot, Leucosia a cousin of Aeneas, Misenus the trumpeter, Prochyta, Caieta Aeneas' nurse. In Virgil's version some of these receive no mention, and Palinurus is lost at sea instead of at the cape named after him. Apart from a briefly recorded halt at Caieta the only port of call between Sicily and the Tiber mouth is Cumae, near Cape Misenum (where Misenus died), at the northern end of the Gulf of Naples, and here the whole action of the sixth book of the poem is set. This concentration is in accordance with Virgil's practice in general in the treatment of the legend; and the choice of Cumae as scene of a principal episode is intelligible for more reasons than one. It was, for instance, in a region closely familiar to Virgil from his frequent residence at Naples near by. It was charged with moving memories of the anxious days of the war against Sextus Pompeius in 38–36 B.C., when it served as a naval base for Octavian's forces, and was the scene of a sea battle and of a fateful conference between the rival commanders. But above all it was seat of an oracle of Apollo and of the celebrated Cumaean Sibyl, and had in its vicinity lake Avernus, supposed to be an entrance to the underworld and location of an oracle where prophecies could be elicited by necromancy from the spirits of the dead. This made it obviously opportune as scene of a counterpart in the *Aeneid* of one of the most spectacular of Homeric episodes, the visit of Ulysses to the underworld which takes place in the eleventh book of the *Odyssey*. It moreover enables this episode to be placed conveniently in the poem, at a point when the Trojans have reached Italy at last and the time has come to evoke the image of future Rome as end and object of the whole story, for which purpose prophecy and revelation need to be employed.

The story of Aeneas' visit to Cumae and his descent into the underworld there falls into two main sections. The first includes the consultation of the hero with the Sibyl, and the death and funeral of Misenus, and the quest for and finding of the Golden Bough; it occupies lines 1–235 of the book. The rest of the book, lines 236–901 (all but the last three), describes the experience of the hero during his descent into the world of the dead.

The first section (1–235) begins with an elaborate description of the reliefs on the temple doors at Cumae, with their story of the Minotaur and Theseus and Ariadne and Daedalus and Icarus, which Aeneas studies as he waits for the Sibyl to appear (1–41). Next follows the consultation of the Sibyl (42–155). In this the thought of Rome is introduced by Aeneas' promise of the later association of the Sibyl's prophecies with the Roman state (in the Sibylline Books); the Sibyl declares that the Trojans' wanderings are now over, and forecasts the coming war in Italy, thus marking a stage of transition in the development of the poem; and Aeneas recalls Anchises' command to him to make the descent into the underworld, so that the reader is kept aware that this will be an act of devotion to Anchises and inspired by him. Finally the Sibyl warns Aeneas of Misenus' death, and instructs him of the necessity of procuring the Golden Bough as passport to the world of the dead and safe return therefrom. The consultation is followed immediately (156–235) by the discovery of the death of Misenus, the finding of the Bough, and the performance of Misenus' funeral rites. The death of Misenus at this point of the Trojans' journey is given by the legend: the description of his funeral rites not only illustrates one aspect of the piety of Aeneas, but also makes an effective preparation for the scenes which are to follow in the world of the dead. The Golden Bough marks Aeneas as a man chosen by destiny.

The second and principal section of the episode (236–898) begins with a preliminary sacrifice at the entrance of the underworld (236–

263), followed by a brief invocation (264–7) and a description of
the progress of the hero, with the Sibyl as guide, through a passage-
way inhabited by evil shapes and spirits to an open space in which
various legendary monsters have their quarters around a huge tree,
roost of deceptive dreams (268–94). The two next approach the
river Acheron and Charon's ferry, and see the shades of the dead
waiting to cross. Aeneas learns that those whose bodies have not
been given due burial must wait a hundred years before they can
pass the river. He sees here sundry of his comrades who have been
lost at sea, and in particular the helmsman Palinurus, lost just
before on the voyage from Sicily to Italy. Palinurus begs to be
taken with Aeneas across the river and is rebuked by the Sibyl for
supposing that entreaties can prevail against the law of the gods.
Aeneas and the Sibyl enter Charon's boat and are ferried over
(295–416). Now (417) they pass the entrance guarded by Cerberus,
whom the Sibyl renders unconscious with a drugged titbit, and
enter (426) a region assigned to various categories of those who have
died prematurely: infants, people executed for crimes they did not
commit, people who had done no wrong but killed themselves for
weariness of life, lovers who died of disappointed love or otherwise of
love's effects. Here Aeneas sees the ghost of Dido and speaks to her,
but she stands silent with averted eyes, and then turns from him, to
join the husband with whom death has reunited her. Next comes
the ghost of Deiphobus, prince of Troy and husband of Helen after
Paris was killed, himself killed and mutilated in a ghastly fashion by
Menelaus at the taking of the city. He tells his story to Aeneas, but
before Aeneas can reply the Sibyl interrupts to say that they must
press on: there is no time for pity or regrets. And now (540) they
have reached a parting of the ways: the way to the right leads to the
palace of the god of the underworld, and past it to Elysium, while
the way to the left leads to the prison house where the worst sinners
are eternally tormented. In the section that follows (548–627)
Aeneas sees the prison house and hears the groans and clanking of
chains: the Sibyl tells him of the fate of the sinners within, the
legendary sinners, such as the giants who warred against the gods,
and Tityos and Ixion and the rest, and the various classes of human
sinners who share their afflictions—those guilty of crimes against
their kin, or of avarice, adultery, treason, rebellion. They pass on
(628), and Aeneas fixes the Golden Bough on the door of the palace
of Pluto and Proserpine. And now (637) they come to the Elysian
fields, bathed in perpetual radiance, where the souls of the virtuous

live at ease, in cool bowers and meadows, amid fragrant odours and sweet music: these are they who have earned their reward not merely by innocence but by achievement, warriors and priests and poets and inventors, all who have deserved by their services to be remembered by mankind. Among them Aeneas finds his father, who shows him (679–888) the plain by the river of Lethe where souls await their birth into the world, explains the doctrine of purgation and re-incarnation, and enumerates and identifies for him a long series of future heroes of Alba Longa and Rome, from Aeneas' own next descendants to Octavian's nephew and heir Marcellus who died (while Virgil was working on the *Aeneid*) in his nineteenth year. This done, and having 'fired Aeneas' heart with the hope of fame to come' (889), Anchises takes Aeneas and the Sibyl to the Gates of Horn and Ivory, through which ghosts and dreams respectively ascend from the world of the dead to the world of the living, and sees them depart through the Gate of Ivory. Thus ends the episode. The Gates of Horn and Ivory are as striking a symbol as the Golden Bough which began it, and their full significance in their context is equally mysterious. The idea comes from the *Odyssey* (19.562–7), where the two gates are specifically the gates of dreams, true dreams and false dreams respectively. In Virgil the distinction seems to be rather between real ghosts—i.e. spirits of the dead revisiting the upper world—and illusory appearances in dreams, but even of this much one cannot be sure.

The story told above is based on the story of Ulysses' experience in the eleventh book of the *Odyssey*, even more closely than a superficial inspection of the two might at first suggest. Ulysses meets first of all an unburied comrade who begs for burial so that his shade can find rest. Next he meets the prophet Teiresias, on whose account he has come, and receives from him a prophecy of the future. Next he meets his own mother. Next, he sees a series of heroines of old legend and hears their stories. Next, he meets figures from his own past; Agamemnon who met a ghastly end on his return home from the Trojan war, and Ajax, once his friend but now embittered, who turns away in silence when addressed. Finally he sees Tityus and Tantalus and other legendary offenders being punished for their sins. The resemblances in the above with Aeneas' encounters with Palinurus, Dido and Deiphobus and the account he hears of the sinners being punished are plain enough. And the order of the encounters is similar too; with the difference that the encounter with Teiresias, cause of Ulysses' adventure, comes first in the *Odyssey*;

whereas the encounter with Anchises, cause of Aeneas' adventure, comes last in the *Aeneid*, so as to form the climax of the episode. It will be noticed also that Anchises as prophet resembles Teiresias, and as parent resembles Ulysses' mother; and further that the pageant of heroines which follows Ulysses' meeting with Teiresias has its counterpart (rather surprisingly) in the pageant of Roman heroes which Anchises shows his son; so that the whole group, Teiresias—mother—heroines, has contributed something to the meeting of Aeneas with his father. The correspondence of Virgil's story with its Homeric 'original' is thus very extensive, despite the completely different effect of it as a whole. Part of this difference results from the blending with the Homeric motifs of motifs derived from other sources which we can also observe.

One of these other motifs is the 'pageant of heroes' which we meet in various contexts in Roman art and literature: the processions of busts of ancestors at the funerals of the nobility, the arrays of statues in public places such as the forum and the Capitol, the enumerations of the names of famous men as examples in the discourses of orators.[1] The pageant of heroes shown to Aeneas by Anchises evidently owes something of its character to the Roman fondness for series and pageants such as these. It owes its setting to a reminiscence of the Myth of Er which concludes the *Republic* of Plato. Er had died and then returned to life, his death having been in the nature of a trance, and was able to report what he had seen in the world of the dead. He told how the souls of men (and animals) alternately live mortal lives on earth in physical bodies and return to the other world between such incarnations for periods of a thousand years; during which time they undergo purgation, if necessary, to cleanse them of blemishes acquired by sin in their last earthly lifetime, before being summoned to begin a new one. They are given a choice of the station and character they shall have in their new incarnation; and then, after drinking the water of Lethe so as to forget their past existence, they are born again in accordance with the choice they have made. Er sees the souls assembled in the meadow by Lethe and watches them make their choices, identifying many famous and infamous characters from legend and history among them. This evidently enough has suggested the setting of the pageant in the *Aeneid*, in which the Roman heroes of the future are seen by Aeneas in the plain by Lethe awaiting their turn to be born. It will be noticed however that there are important differences of detail and application. The souls in the Republic do not come to Lethe or abandon their former personalities until the time of their rebirth is due; but most of the souls exhibited in the *Aeneid* will have to wait for many hundreds of years before they are born again into this world, though apparently they have already drunk the Lethe-water and discarded their former personalities. Further, while the souls in the *Republic* are seen in the characters which they had acquired in maturity in their former lives, before they make their new choices and drink Lethe, those in the *Aeneid* are seen endowed already with the personalities and physical attributes of their future lives, regardless of the fact that they will start these lives as babies. Lastly, the whole intention of the story in the *Republic* is as a moral warning: that we should take care of our souls in this life so that when we come to make the fatal choice of our next one we choose with a pure and unclouded judgement. In the *Aeneid* there is no fatal choice, and the purpose of the story is simply to enable Aeneas, and the reader, to have a vision of the future splendour of Rome to which the story of the *Aeneid* is leading, the end and object of the hero's vocation.

This revelation of the purpose which Aeneas has been called to serve is communicated by Anchises as an inspiration and encouragement to him. This was Anchises' promise when he appeared to his son in the dream in the fifth book and told him to venture the descent into the underworld: 'then you shall learn all the story of your posterity, and what this city is that is promised to you' (5.737). This is the moral that he draws in the course of his commentary on the pageant: 'And now do we hesitate to exert in action all that we have of strength and courage? Or does fear hold us back from standing for our right in Italy?' (6.806–7). And the effect of the revelation corresponds to its intention: 'and when he had shown his son all these things, and fired his heart with the promise of fame to come ...' (889). The speech of Anchises and the vision that it accompanies are thus protreptic in their intention and effect, an exhortation to effort and endurance. And in this there is a reminiscence of another speech in literature addressed in a vision by a Roman to his successor, the speech of the elder to the younger Scipio Africanus in the so-called Dream of Scipio which forms the sixth book of Cicero's treatise *On the State*, Cicero's essay at a Platonic myth in his Latin counterpart to Plato's *Republic*. In this the young Scipio, later to be the final conqueror of Carthage, has a dream in which the elder Scipio appears and shows him the order of the universe and the nature of the human soul, and how the spirits of those who have served the state well can earn by their virtue and achievement a permanent escape from imprisonment in the body; ascending into a heavenly region they will dwell there in felicity with other blessed spirits. Echoes of this speech can be felt in Anchises' speech in Virgil, where he speaks of the origin of the soul in the fiery breath that permeates the universe and of the concept of the body as a kind of prison of the soul, and these, together with the fact that the setting is a vision and the speaker a forebear appearing in a vision, make it plain that Virgil has the Dream of Scipio in mind.[2] The purpose of the revelation and the discourse which accompanies it is protreptic in both cases; to fire Aeneas 'with the hope of fame to come', and to make Scipio 'more zealous still in defence of the State'.[3] But a difference of motive will be noticed, in that the incentive offered to Scipio is primarily the reward of his own virtue after death, whereas the incentive offered to Aeneas is the greatness of the future of his people.

The Homeric basis of Virgil's episode has thus been modified, in the process of its re-working, by the infusion of echoes of Roman custom and by reminiscences of famous passages in Plato and Cicero, as well as by the personal story of Aeneas which forms its new context; and what can be seen of the process in this instance is a good example of the kaleidoscopic working of Virgil's imagination.

Another modification of the Homeric framework arises, obviously enough, from the fact that in Virgil's account the hero enters and passes through the underworld, whereas in Homer's he stands at the edge and waits for the ghosts to come to him in succession, attracted by the blood of the sacrifice which he has offered. Hence in Homer the underworld has no topography, but in Virgil it has one. It is of course unlikely that any standard and official conception of the underworld existed in Virgil's time; for there was no official theology to provide one, and individual poets no doubt created their own from assorted literary reminiscences and their own imaginations. Nor of course would the conceptions of the after-life, if any, held by moderately sophisticated people correspond literally to these poetic pictures, any more than such people's conception of the Olympian gods would correspond to the picture given in the Homeric poems and developed later by a whole succession of poets. But ancient literary references to the underworld do, we know, exhibit a number of recurrent features: Charon's ferry and the crossing of the infernal river, the three-headed dog Cerberus who guards the entry, the king and queen of the underworld, Pluto and Proserpine, the judges of the dead, the torments of the damned, the abode of the blessed in the Elysian fields. These features all occur in Virgil's version, but some of them which elsewhere enjoy most prominence are in Virgil subordinated and receive only brief mention: for instance, the king and queen of the underworld, and the activity of the judges of the dead. On the other hand two conceptions assume importance in Virgil's picture which are not among the familiar features that recur constantly elsewhere. One of these is the cyclic reincarnation of souls and their assembly in the meadow by Lethe in preparation for rebirth, of which something has been said above. Obviously this could not be a part of any general conception of the underworld, because belief in reincarnation was not a general belief. The second less familiar feature is the assignment of separate regions to special categories of souls other than those of the unburied, the damned, and the blessed. This feature, like that of the souls awaiting rebirth in the meadow, is important to the development of the episode in the *Aeneid*, as it is in such a special region or regions that Aeneas has his moving encounters with Dido and Deiphobus. It seems to reflect an idea, of which we learn only through a few incidental references in ancient authors, that the prematurely dead must wander without finding rest until they reach the age at which they would have died in the normal course.[4] The idea that this sojourn in a species of limbo is temporary seems indeed necessary to Virgil's story if there is not to be a contradiction with the idea of reincarnation which he later introduces; and the classes of souls mentioned at this point are in fact all victims of premature death—infants, suicides, those put to death unjustly (since the justly executed would stand to be punished as sinners in a separate category), and those dead for love. But the poet says nothing of their stay in limbo being temporary; and when he comes to the group which includes Deiphobus, the warriors, he seems no longer to be following the concept of a category of the prematurely dead.[5] For these are not described as 'the slain in war' (and so prematurely dead) but as 'famous warriors' (478), and they include one—Adrastus—who is celebrated in legend as *survivor* of the battle at Thebes in which his comrades fell; moreover, he and others of them belong to a past generation, and would by now have been released from limbo if their stay there were determined by the normal span of human life. Thus the conception of a limbo for the prematurely dead, like that of the reincarnation of souls, provides the setting for a moving and effective scene—in this case the encounters with Dido and Deiphobus—and Virgil's literary motive for adopting it is clear enough. But neither conception is treated in a way that might lead us to think that it was part of any coherent doctrinal scheme in the poet's mind.

It will be seen from this that Virgil's picture of the underworld has been created in the same way as his version of the story of Aeneas in the poem as a whole. The process involves a very free selection and adaptation of elements from a traditional version and its variants, in combination with motifs derived primarily from Homer but also from other sources of literary reminiscence, and the fusion of the whole in the imagination of the poet. The resulting story of Aeneas' fortunes in the poem as a whole does not correspond either to any pre-existing version of the legend, nor to a supposed historical truth. Similarly Virgil's picture of the underworld in the sixth book must not be expected to correspond either to any received traditional account or to Virgil's own explicit belief. It is not primarily a religious document, and apart from its quality as a splendid and moving counterpart to a great Homeric episode its functions in the poem are to emphasize the role of the hero's dead father as comfort and inspiration to his son, and to introduce the first of the two prophetic revelations of a distant future which express, with the emotional impact of direct vision, the significance of Aeneas' story as the beginning of the history of Rome.

But if we cannot expect to find in this book any clear indication of the poet's beliefs, we do find in it an expression of certain feelings which are disclosed elsewhere in the poem and here seem to acquire a certain emphasis from the repetition of the motifs which convey them. The first of these is the sense of the harshness of the world order in its dealings with men. Repeatedly the poet in his own or his hero's person remarks on this as he pities the 'cruel lot' of the unburied, the 'cruel fate' of Dido, the 'harsh doom' which has condemned Marcellus already to an untimely death. He dwells, now expressly, now by implication, on the innocence of the sufferers and on the inflexible sternness of the law which ordains their suffering: 'cease to suppose that the divine decree can be changed by prayer' (376), 'how much they wish . . .: but the divine ordinance forbids and the dread water's grim expanse prevents escape' (436–9).

A chosen few like Aeneas are favoured by heaven and raised by exceptional endowment above the ordinary limitations of mortality. A chosen few like Anchises attain a lasting peace and happiness in Elysium. It is the reward of high achievement, and achievement must be man's aim in life, achievement especially in the service of his fellow men. 'And do we yet hesitate to show our worth in deeds?'

says Anchises to his son, as Jupiter later will comment that 'to win honour by achievement is manhood's work' as he watches Pallas go to meet his death (10.468–9). This is the sentiment of the Homeric heroes: 'let me not die without effort, without honour, but first do some great deed that men to come shall hear of' (*Iliad*, 22.304–5); and it had been the sentiment of generations of Romans, in the context not merely of individual achievement but of the service of the state. Aeneas is a hero in both the Homeric and the Roman tradition. But it is manifest that he is not propelled by the spontaneous vitality of the Homeric heroes or of the Roman heroes of the past. Homer's Achilles when Ulysses met him in the underworld would accept the condition of a serf to be alive again; Virgil's Aeneas as he sees the souls that await rebirth wonders with pity at their strange desire, their fatal yearning for the light of day (721). We have seen that in all the poem he is summoned on by a call that overrules his private feelings for others as well as for himself, and in this book the urgency of the call is personified in the figure of the Sibyl: 'this is no time for gazing . . .' (37), 'make haste, make haste . . .' (51), 'Aeneas, night draws near, and we let pass the time with weeping' (539). Precisely what it is that the Sibyl symbolizes the poet has left the reader to divine for himself.

He has left it also to the reader to divine the significance for himself of other potentially symbolic elements in this episode: the descent to the shades which is subject of the whole, the arms of the ghosts outstretched toward the inaccessible further shore, the Golden Bough, the Ivory Gate. Is the descent to the shades ordeal, initiation, revelation, preparation? Are the Bough and the Gate, which enclose the episode, more than the credential of Aeneas' vocation at the beginning of the story and a reminder at its end that this is a living man who emerges from the world of the dead? In Homer, as was earlier remarked, the Gates of Horn and Ivory are the gates of truthful and deceiving dreams respectively. In Virgil the language of the poet leaves it obscure whether the distinction is the same as in Homer or is a new and different distinction, between the gate through which real ghosts pass to revisit the world of life and that through which are sent the illusions which are dreams. As for the Bough, in this there is, to be sure, a reminiscence of the bough that the challenger of the king of the grove at Nemi must pluck to be token of his right to challenge, and a reminiscence too of the Golden Fleece, gleaming among the leaves of the oak-tree in the Colchian forest. The poet himself compares the Bough (205) to the mistletoe with its golden berries; and it is not an extravagant fancy to suppose that he knew of the religious awe with which the mistletoe was regarded by the Druids of Gaul, who would allow it to be cut only with a golden knife, and believed that it marked as divinely chosen the tree on which it grew. Some again have seen in the Bough the wand carried by the initiates at the Eleusinian Mysteries, and some the golden palm carried and dedicated by a Roman conqueror, and some again a recollection of the phrase applied in Meleager's Garland to the poems of Plato—a spray or bough of gold.[6] All or any of these associations may have been present somewhere in Virgil's conscious or sub-conscious mind; and more than that we are not likely ever to know.

X

ECHOES OF HISTORY

As has been said, the Aeneid is not only the first chapter of Rome's history, but also contains anticipations of later chapters of that history, partly in the form of various kinds of prophetic revelation, and partly by exhibiting within its own story distinctive customs and institutions still familiar in the Roman scene in the poet's own day. But there is another way additional to these in which the story told in the poem acquires an extended significance, and this is the evocation of later events through analogy, sometimes pointed by a strikingly allusive phrase or detail. This kind of significance by analogy may attach to the whole story, or to whole sections of it, or to particular incidents in it.

Thus the hero's trials and labours are evidently illustrative of the effort and sacrifice of Romans down the ages in the service of the Roman state: *tantae molis erat Romanam condere gentem* can describe the whole of the people's history, as well as the experience of its founder in particular. The hero's virtues likewise, his courage and sense of duty and reverence for the gods, are expressive of the moral values of the Roman tradition. Conversely, the people who are broken through their resistance to the hero's mission are representative of the cost to others of the fulfilment of Rome's destiny; and their fates are commemorated, as we have seen, not without sympathy and admiration. This kind of illustrative significance runs right through the story as a whole. It runs also through the principal subordinate movements of the story, the Carthaginian episode and the war in Italy, with an allusiveness that is not systematic and may take more directions than one. Dido's resistance to the plan of fate for Rome reflects the conflict between the destinies of Rome and Carthage, and her curse anticipates the deadly enmity which worked itself out in the Punic wars.[1] But the story of Dido's dangerous love and Aeneas' temporary involvement with it must inevitably have evoked for the Roman reader of Virgil's time the recent memory of Cleopatra, another African queen whose love entangled a Roman leader and seemed to threaten Rome with subordination to a foreign power, and whose personal magnitude none the less excited even her enemies' admiration. The memory was too recent and the analogy too clear not to be felt, and the sense of it appears in details of Virgil's story: the glimpses that he gives us of the two lovers abandoned to their private pleasures and 'forgetful of honour', of Aeneas' purple raiment and jewelled sword—these are reflections, in less vivid but more seemly terms, of what we read of Cleopatra and Antony in Plutarch; and Virgil's phrase 'pale with foreboding of death' in his description of Cleopatra after Actium on the prophetic shield in the eighth book is closely similar to a phrase that he has used of Dido in the fourth.[2] Again, the story of the war in Italy, between combatants destined to be united afterwards in perpetual amity, has features which evoke on the one hand the conquest of the Italian peoples by Rome, which ended in a partnership, and on the other hand the civil war, which ended in the *pax Augusta*. At the beginning of the poem Jupiter prophesies that Aeneas in the war in Italy will 'subdue proud peoples and impose order on them', and again elsewhere speaks of him as called 'to govern Italy, big with promise of empire and angry murmuring of war';[3] and though this idea of a civilizing conqueror is not developed in the story that follows it is implied more than once in scenes where the Italians are depicted as primitive and raw in their valour by contrast with the Trojans: for instance in the account of the robber chieftain Ufens in the catalogue of tribes in the seventh book, or the boasts of Numanus in the ninth.[4] At the same time there is the quite separate analogy with the civil war. The Latins are divided among themselves. The war is an *infandum bellum, arma impia*, product of *furor* and *violentia*— all terms with very strong and recent associations when Virgil wrote.[5] The war ends with the promise of reconciliation through the moderation of the victor. These analogies would be felt by any reader in the decade following the battle of Actium. Nevertheless they are not precise but reflect general conceptions in the poet's mind which appear intermittently and overlap sometimes with one another.

There is also a preciser kind of analogy between particular situations, the sense of which may suggest to the poet a word or phrase which in turn directs the awareness of the reader to that which suggested it. For instance, in the seventh book Juno resolves to provoke war between the Latins and Trojans, moved by the spiteful wish to delay the marriage, which she knows she cannot prevent, of Aeneas with Latinus' daughter. In her angry soliloquy she exclaims *hac socer atque gener coeant mercede suorum*, which may be freely translated 'let this be the price their people pay (in blood) for the pact of marriage between these two'.[6] The expression 'these two' here represents the Latin phrase *socer atque gener* = 'father-in-law and son-in-law', poetically intractable in English but correctly describing Latinus father of the princess and Aeneas her prospective husband. This phrase, fully appropriate to the context in which it stands, had also strong and unescapable associations of a different kind for Virgil's readers: it was a stock phrase for Caesar and Pompey, who stood in precisely this relationship to one another, and whose conflict had generated the recent civil wars. Already in Catullus the two are *socer generque*, and in the *Aeneid* itself elsewhere they are *socer* and *gener* also.[7] The associations of the phrase are of course reinforced by the fact that the war impending between Latins and Trojans is thought of here as an affliction brought on the ordinary citizens, like the civil war, by the dissensions of the great and powerful. And these associations have suggested to the poet the choice (whether consciously or not) of a verb which is ambiguous; for *coeant* can mean either 'come together in agreement' or 'come together in collision'.[8] As a result Juno's imprecation can bear a second meaning alternative to that which it naturally bears in its context; it can mean 'let this be the price their people pay for the conflict of these two', evoking with the phrase *socer atque gener* the thought of the civil wars of Rome at the outset of the *infandum bellum* of the *Aeneid*. The double meaning could not be lost on a contemporary of the poet, but it does not follow that it is an effect which he has sought: it is more likely to have arisen by the same kind of sub-conscious associative process which in the ordinary mind produces the accidental pun.

Sub-conscious association, though of a rather different kind, must also have been at work in the following case. After describing, in the second book of the *Aeneid*, the death of Priam the poet dwells on the contrast between the old king's squalid and miserable end and the glories of his former state, 'proud master of so many peoples and so many kings, lord of all Asia'.[9] Then he proceeds: 'there lies the mighty trunk upon the shore, the head torn from the shoulders, a nameless corpse'. The word 'shore' is strange in this context, for the setting of the scene is Priam's own palace; it has surely come into the poet's mind from the memory of another scene which it at once recalls, one which had made a profound impression on Virgil's generation. This was the end of Pompey, once the greatest general in the world, conqueror of Asia for the Roman Republic, and later leader of the Republic's army against Caesar, turned by his defeat at Pharsalus into a helpless fugitive, and murdered by treachery as he was about to land in Egypt as suppliant of the Egyptian king. The words of Plutarch's account of this are themselves a commentary on the end of Virgil's description of the death of Priam: 'so they cut off Pompey's head and threw the rest of his body overboard, leaving it naked upon the shore'.[10] And the way in which the thought of Pompey has come into the poet's mind can be understood by setting his description of Priam as 'proud master of so many peoples and so many kings, lord of all Asia' against Appian's enumeration of the eastern contingents in the camp of Pompey before Pharsalus: 'all the peoples of the East . . . were in Pompey's army: Thracians, Hellespontians, Bithynians, Phrygians, Ionians, Lydians, Pamphylians, Pisidians, Paphlagonians; Cilicians, Syrians, Phoenicians, the Hebrews and their neighbours the Arabs; Cyprians and Rhodians, Cretan slingers, and all the other islanders. Kings and princes were there in person, leading their own troops.'[11] Here the analogy between the fortunes of Priam and Pompey seems to have affected the poet so forcibly that the images of the two have become confounded in his thought, forcing the word 'shore' into a context to which it does not properly belong. That word in its turn guides the reader's mind to the analogy, and enables him to feel some of the significance which it has added to the end of Priam in Virgil's imagination.

In the two examples just quoted the perception of the analogy was very likely unmeditated. In others a conscious intention seems to have been at work. When Aeneas arrives, in Book 8, outside the settlement which the Arcadian Evander has established on the site where Rome will later stand, he finds the inhabitants making sacrifice to Hercules at the Ara Maxima, the Great Altar, a monument which still existed in the poet's own time and was still the scene of a sacrifice to Hercules. Aeneas learns from Evander that the sacrifice is an act of thanksgiving, performed because Hercules had killed a fire-breathing giant named Cacus by whom the little settlement had formerly been terrorized. The story of Hercules and Cacus was a part of the legend of Evander inherited by Virgil, and the Ara Maxima was an obvious feature to introduce into an episode which had for one of its objects to make felt the presence of historical Rome in the prehistoric setting of the story. It stands therefore in the poem in its own right. But it is treated with an evident and purposeful consciousness of an analogy between Hercules and the younger Caesar, Octavian, victor of Actium and restorer of peace to the Roman world. Both are performers of prodigious feats, both are benefactors of mankind, liberating the world from terrors and oppressors and making it possible for life to be lived in peace. Some contemporaries of Virgil saw in Cacus, the robber monster of the legend, a symbol of marauding Alpine tribes who once harried the north of Italy, marauders quelled by Octavian in the years preceding his final struggle with Antony.[12] Virgil himself in his picture of the battle of Actium on the prophetic shield imagines a menacing company of monstrous Egyptian gods arrayed on the side of Antony and Cleopatra; and Propertius writing a few years later calls the young Caesar, in the same context of the Actian victory, *mundi servator*, 'saviour of the world'.[13] Hence when Evander tells his guest that his people and he are making their sacrifice as an act of thanksgiving for being 'saved' from the monster, *servati facimus*,[14] the words would bring the analogy of Octavian's achievement to mind; and when he says further that in the fullness of time 'a god came at last' to their aid this would suggest the same analogy with the leader already called a god by Virgil in the *Eclogues* and given the attributes of a god by him in the *Georgics*.[15] Horace too, writing some time between 27 and 23 B.C., imagines the young Caesar in the company of Hercules and the other typical 'saviour' gods, Castor and Pollux.[16] Thus there is no doubt that Virgil approaches the composition of this whole episode with the parallelism between Hercules and Octavian in mind. And in the latter part of it he points the parallelism by what appear to be deliberate echoes, in the account of the honours paid by the Arcadians to Hercules, of honours paid by the Romans to Octavian on a very famous occasion. After his victory at Actium and settlement of affairs in Egypt and Asia it was decreed among other compliments that libations should be poured in his honour both at public and at private banquets, and that his name should be inserted in the ancient hymn chanted by the dancing priests called Salii, one of the most venerable institutions of Roman public worship.[17] In Virgil's story the recital of the tale of Hercules and Cacus by Evander is immediately followed by the pouring of libations to Hercules, and this in turn is followed shortly afterwards by the appearance of two parties of Salii who sing a hymn commemorating the labours of the god and the untiring courage with which he faced and overcame them. The mention of the libations alone would not necessarily be significant, but here there is also the highly distinctive motif of the Salian hymn to complete the analogy with the honours of Octavian. Moreover, this motif is not one that would normally offer itself to the poet's mind, since the Salii were not normally associated with the worship of Hercules at Rome: it has therefore all the appearance of having been deliberately sought. That the consul Valerius Potitus who sacrificed on behalf of the senate and people to give thanks for Octavian's return in 29 B.C. bore a name nearly resembling that of the Potitii, hereditary priests of the Great Altar of Hercules in early times, was a coincidence; but this coincidence too has been exploited in Virgil's story, where a Potitius is twice mentioned, with special emphasis, as leader of the ceremonies. It has been noted too that Octavian's triumph in 29 B.C. began on the day following the annual sacrifice to Hercules at the Great Altar, whether by accident or design we do not know. It is clear in any case that the figure of Hercules the saviour whose story Aeneas hears on his arrival at the site of Rome is meant to evoke by analogy the thought of Octavian. At the end of the same book of the *Aeneid* the scenes on the prophetic shield show Octavian's victory at Actium over the menace of Egyptian domination, and the thanksgiving of the people for their deliverance.

The following is another case in which the events in the story seem chosen deliberately to bring contemporary events to mind, and again the person concerned is the young Caesar. In the fifth book of the poem Aeneas, after leaving Carthage, is brought back by an accident of the weather to the place in north-west Sicily where his father Anchises had died a year before. He takes the occasion to hold funeral games in his father's honour. These are an evident counterpart of the games held by Achilles for Patroclus in the twenty-third book of *Iliad*, just as the subsequent descent of Aeneas into the underworld is a counterpart of the visit of Ulysses to the world of the dead in the eleventh book of the *Odyssey*. But games were also a Roman institution; and it happens that Octavian on two highly significant occasions held games in honour of his father (by adoption) Julius Caesar. The first of these was in July of 44 B.C., at the very outset of his career, only a few months after Caesar's murder, when as Caesar's heir he gave the games variously called *Victoriae Caesaris* or *Veneris Genetricis* on his behalf.[18] The second was at the end of the civil wars, when he dedicated in 29 B.C. the temple called *Divi Iuli* to the now deified Caesar and held games to celebrate the dedication.[19] The analogy between these acts of piety and that of Aeneas would suggest itself readily enough to a contemporary, and that it was intended to do so appears from two sets of facts. At the beginning of the episode Aeneas speaks of Anchises as his *divinus parens*, which here can hardly mean anything but that his father is now a god, just as *divina mater* is said of the goddess Cybele in Lucretius.

He then goes on to pray that his father may grant him to perform the same act of worship annually henceforth, 'when our city is settled and I have dedicated a temple to him'.[20] The point of these phrases is mysterious as they stand, but becomes easily intelligible on the assumption that they have been suggested to the poet's imagination by an analogy in his mind between the honours paid by Aeneas to Anchises and those paid by Octavian to the deified Julius Caesar after the final cessation of the Civil War. This assumption is confirmed by strongly distinctive occurrences in the last two events of Aeneas' games for Anchises which correspond with distinctive occurrences that we hear of in Octavian's games for Julius. The final event in the games in the *Aeneid* is an archery contest. In this the dove which serves as target is shot down before the last competitor, the Trojans' host Acestes, can have his turn. Left without a target he shoots an arrow as high as he can into the air to show his strength and skill; whereupon the arrow catches fire in its flight and vanishes leaving a trail of fire behind it.[21] This is described in elaborately mysterious terms as a portent of great and awful events to come in the still distant future. Next, the young sons of the Trojans appear on horseback, led by Ascanius, and give a display of equestrian drill, a performance familiar in later Rome under the name *Lusus Troiae*. Now, we are specifically told that the *Lusus Troiae* was one of the events included in the games given by Octavian at the dedication of the temple for his deified father in 29 B.C.;[22] it was in fact a performance in which he took a personal interest, 'thinking it good as a matter of policy that the rising generation of the Roman nobility should be encouraged to do themselves honour in public in this way'.[23] And at the games of 44 B.C. a great sensation was caused by the appearance of a comet, taken by the populace as proof of Julius Caesar's divinity (they thought it was his soul departing to the sky to be with the other gods), and by Octavian himself as an omen of his own success.[24] This comet is described by Ovid in his *Metamorphoses* in terms very similar to those used by Virgil in his description of what happens to Acestes' arrow, though Virgil for obvious reasons makes the arrow turn into a shooting star rather than a comet; in both descriptions the central idea is of something that takes fire in its passage through the sky, in the one case Caesar's soul, in the other Acestes' arrow.[25] Thus the portent in the *Aeneid* recalls the games of 44 B.C. and the performance of the *Lusus Troiae* recalls the games of 29; and this recollection of honours paid by Octavian to his father Caesar explains the references to Anchises as *divinus* and awaiting the dedication of a temple, and establishes the analogy between the filial piety of Aeneas and the filial piety of Octavian. For the theme of the piety of son to father is of course what is illustrated by the games of the fifth book of the *Aeneid*, and this has its counterpart in the inspiration which the father affords to the son: presently Anchises' ghost will bring comfort to Aeneas in his moment of discouragement and promise the revelation of the purpose of his mission which is to be given him in the underworld in the following book. To Octavian too his *pietas* was an inspiration to action, 'to avenge his father's death', 'to fulfil his policies', and 'to achieve the honours that he had achieved'.[26]

In the instances cited above it is possible to show not only that there is an analogy between something in contemporary history and something in the *Aeneid* story, but also that this analogy has been felt by the poet, sometimes also sought by him. In other cases analogy is evident but uncertainty may remain whether it has been sought or felt by the poet. Here are two examples, both relating to notable occasions in the year 27 B.C. In that year Octavian professed to relinquish his absolute powers and restore the traditional authority of senate and people. 'I restore all to you, armies, laws, government of the provinces'; so he is made to say on the occasion by a later historian, in a speech which may well (though this cannot be proved) be founded on a contemporary report.[27] In the sequel a number of fresh honours were conferred upon him: he received the title of 'Augustus', an oak-wreath was to be suspended permanently over the entrance to his house, and a golden shield commemorating his virtues was dedicated in the senate-chamber.[28] The act of apparent magnanimity which elicited these honours has a parallel in the magnanimity of Aeneas at the end of the *Aeneid*, when he declares that if he is victorious he will not ask for any privileges for himself from his victory or disturb the authority of the Latin king: 'Let Latinus', he says, 'keep command of the army, let him keep the powers that are traditionally his.'[29] The precise insistence here on *control of the armed forces* as basis of political power may seem to reflect a way of thinking that belongs in fact to the world of real politics rather than to the world of poetry; and if this is so, the phrase 'keep command of the army' will be due to an echo of words used by Octavian in 27 B.C., and the analogy between the occasion in the poem and the occasion in history will be more than a simple coincidence. The phrase is distinctive; and the event was remarkable, and occurred moreover precisely at the time when the *Aeneid* was being written. Nor is this the only example of apparent analogy between a distinctive occurrence of 27 B.C. and a distinctive feature of the *Aeneid* story. At the end of the eighth book of the *Aeneid* the hero's mother Venus brings him arms made for him by Vulcan, chief among which, and elaborately described, is the famous shield adorned with prophetic scenes from Roman history. All this (except the prophetic and specifically Roman character of the decoration) has its obvious origin in a celebrated episode in the eighteenth book of the *Iliad*; and the non-Homeric element, the prophetic decoration, has its functional and structural counterpart in the *Aeneid* itself, in the prophetic pageant of Roman heroes seen by Aeneas in the underworld in Book 6. Thus it is by no means necessary to look for an origin of the shield of Aeneas in the famous shield, already mentioned, which was dedicated in honour of Octavian in 27 B.C. Equally it is certain that the analogy between the two could not escape the poet's readers or the poet himself; for the dedication of the shield of honour was a notable event, and Octavian (now Augustus) is himself the principal figure on the shield of Aeneas, the description of which was composed after the dedication of the historical shield, as the use of the title Augustus in the description shows; moreover both the shields are of gold. When Venus brings the shield to Aeneas in the *Aeneid* she sets it down 'under an oak', and perhaps it is not fanciful to suppose that the phrase was suggested to the poet's conscious or sub-conscious mind by the oak-wreath which was associated with the shield in the honours decreed for Octavian in 27 B.C. The oak-wreath was awarded 'for saving the lives of fellow-citizens' (*ob cives servatos*); and it will be recalled that it was for 'saving' them that the citizens of Pallanteum are honouring Hercules (*servati facimus meritosque novamus honores*) when Aeneas comes to them at the beginning of this same book which ends with his receiving the shield.

The examples given above have been given to illustrate a fact about the *Aeneid*, the fact of the reflection in it of events and persons in Roman history, and especially of events and persons, and feelings too, that belonged to the poet's own time. Such reflection is not as a rule the outcome of a systematic process, nor always of a conscious intention on the part of the poet. Nor can the extent to which it is carried be adequately judged by us, because so little, after all, is accessible to us of the history of that age. It would therefore be unprofitable to attempt a comprehensive study of the subject here; though some further possible examples are considered in Appendix 5 below. It will have been noticed in any case that these reflections

I V A—H

and allusions do not all enhance in the same degree the poetic effect
for the modern reader of the passages in which they occur. For him
equations such as Hercules = Octavian or Aeneas = Octavian are
perhaps of limited emotional interest. But it is different with the
evocation of the memory of Pompey in the scene of Priam's death,
and different too with the lines which follow the description of
Aeneas' shield and bring the eighth book to a close. As Aeneas takes
up the shield he is said to 'lift on his shoulders the fame and fortunes
of his children's children'.[30] This in its first meaning is of course a
figure of speech for taking up the shield which we have just heard
described, with the scenes from Roman history depicted on it. With
the sentence thus understood the expression 'children's children' has
a double value, with respect to Aeneas: in a common metaphorical
sense it means the Roman people, and in its literal sense it means the
Julian family, supposed to be descended directly from Aeneas
through Ascanius-Iulus and the Alban kings. Thus there is a reference in general to the events in Roman history represented on the
shield and in particular to Octavian's victory at Actium which is the
last and most impressive of them. This however is not the only
double value in the sentence; for 'lifting on his shoulders' at once
suggests the taking up of a burden, and invites us to see in Aeneas'
action a symbol of his role in all the poem, as bearer of responsibility
for the future of his people, the burden indicated at the outset of the
story in the key words *tantae molis erat Romanam condere gentem*. Nor
when this is said is the content of the sentence exhausted. For the
analogy of the shield of Aeneas with the shield dedicated in honour
of Octavian-Augustus suggests analogy between the two persons, and
so the thought that Augustus in Virgil's own day has borne and
bears the same responsibility for his people's future that Aeneas bore
before him. All these ideas are brought to mind as the story
approaches its climax in the fight for Italy which is to occupy the
last books of the poem.

XI

RELEVANT AND IRRELEVANT
ASSOCIATIONS. CONCLUSION

THE *Aeneid* is full of echoes, is constantly recalling or suggesting things both internal and external to itself. Some of the latter lie outside the sphere of the poet's own direct recollection, conscious or unconscious, and belong to the common experience of humanity or to the experience of the later world which Virgil helped to shape. Others spring demonstrably from the recollection of the poet, and three varieties of these have been illustrated in the preceding chapters. There are echoes of earlier literature, poetry and prose, most obviously and pervasively of course from Homer, but also from Ennius and Apollonius and many others. There are echoes of the *Aeneid* itself within the *Aeneid*, and also from Virgil's earlier works the *Eclogues* and the *Georgics*. And there are echoes from Roman legend and history, up to and including the poet's own time.

In some of the examples which have been considered in earlier chapters it is apparent that the echo or repetition is deliberate. This can be affirmed when there is something about it too distinctive to be explicable as due to accident or to purely sub-conscious recall. Thus the resemblance between the Virgilian Games of *Aeneid* 5 and the Homeric Games of *Iliad* 23 (to take a single instance of the ubiquitous recollections of Homer) is not confined to the general motif but extends to the four several events that are its components. The prophetic pageants which end the sixth and the eighth books stand out in the poem through the distinctive similarity of their content and function, and moreover form part of a pattern of duplications marked by the two interventions of Venus, the two interventions of Juno and the two comforting and action-prompting dreams, in all of which in their turn the similarity of basic motif is accompanied by equally distinctive similarities of detail. Again, the games with which Aeneas honours Anchises recall the games with which Octavian on two occasions honoured Caesar, by including two remarkable features which correspond to events distinctive of those occasions; and the poet's awareness of this correspondence (which could not indeed at that moment of history pass unnoticed either by himself or by his readers) is confirmed by turns of phrasing which would be hard to explain on any other hypothesis.

In these and similar cases the emphatic nature of the echo or repetition implies a purpose to achieve some effect by it. Thus, one effect of the re-working of Homeric situations was no doubt to establish a rapport with the reader, to whom the Homeric poems would as a rule be fully familiar. Another was to express the character of Virgil's poem as the Roman successor of the *Iliad* and *Odyssey*: the comparison discloses both the Homeric parentage of Virgil's poetry and its specifically Roman quality at the same time. On the other hand, the effect aimed at in internal repetitions such as that of the pageant motif in the middle of the poem seems to be partly one of emphasis—to throw an important idea into relief; and partly one of formal artistry—to give that part of the poem an architectural kind of structure somewhat as Catullus gave an architectural structure to his sixty-fourth poem, his tableau of the wedding of Peleus and Thetis. And different again from this must be the purpose of the recollections of Octavian's tributes to Caesar in the funeral games held by Aeneas for Anchises: these expressly invite the reader to feel an analogy between the hero of the *Aeneid* and Octavian-Augustus, at least in the immediate context of the devotion of son to father. The emergence of this analogy at other places in the poem has been mentioned in the preceding chapter and will be discussed further in Appendix 5. But it is certainly not sustained at the same level throughout; it is remote, for instance, in the story of the fall of Troy, and the wanderings, and the episode at Carthage.

But while some of the echoes and repetitions in the *Aeneid* can be seen to reflect an intention, and thus to give the value of 'allusions' to the passages where they occur, it is equally evident that many such echoes, whether of motif or of diction, occur without any intention behind them: the poet uses a phrase or an idea that comes to his mind from past literature or legend or from another passage in his own poem simply because it is apt to the requirements of his present context and without any purpose to recall the context from which it has come to him. This may well be true of many detailed reminiscences of Homer. It can be illustrated here with reminiscences of Apollonius. One of the most moving similes in the *Aeneid* is that in which Aeneas' first glimpse of Dido in the half-light of the underworld is compared to the young moon faintly glimpsed through clouds.[1] This is based on a simile of Apollonius which refers to Hercules seen a great way off by one of his companions.[2] Virgil could not be unaware of the origin of his comparison, and equally can have had no intention to recall it in the new context. In another celebrated simile the troubled thoughts of Aeneas as war threatens are compared to the rapidly shifting reflexions of light from the swaying surface of water in a cauldron.[3] This is based on a simile of Apollonius in which the thing illustrated is the agitated heart of Medea torn by love and fear and shame.[4] Here again awareness of the original context could not in any way assist the new one. Similarly, Aeneas' words to Dido in the underworld *invitus, regina, tuo de litore cessi* ('it was not of my own will, highness, that I left your shore') carry no allusion to the context in which (with one word different) they originally were framed, the apology of the Lock of Berenice for leaving the queen's head to become a constellation, in Catullus' translation from the Greek of Callimachus.[5]

It is the same with internal echoes. The distinctive phrase *at domus interior* . . . begins both the description of the feast in Dido's palace and the description of the sight that meets the eyes of the attackers as they burst into Priam's palace;[6] the distinctive phrase *iam pridem resides animos* is used both of Dido's heart unstirred by love since the death of her first husband and of the spirit of the Italians unstirred by warlike excitement for many years before the coming of the Trojans;[7] the distinctive phrase *nova lux oculis offulsit* said of a miraculous illumination of the sky in one passage recurs in another, with a change of one letter and a consequent change of construction (*oculis effulsit*), to describe the glaring eyes of the berserk Turnus.[8] In none of these instances does the one context gain anything from recall of the other. When Aeneas and Turnus are compared to bulls fighting for mastery of the herd the description repeats with one word changed a line from the description in the third *Georgic* of bulls fighting for a heifer *illi inter sese multa vi proelia miscent*; the new context is self-contained and draws nothing useful from the associations of the old one.[9] And as with phrases, so with motifs, it is common for the poet's imagination to repeat itself without any question of the two passages standing in any significant relation one to another. Aeneas admires scenes depicted on temple doors at Carthage and again at Cumae; Neptune rides in his chariot over the sea after the storm in the first book and before the voyage from Sicily to Italy in the fifth; Aeneas retraces his steps through the darkness to look for lost Creusa, and Nisus later retraces his steps through the darkness to look for lost Euryalus; Aeneas in the second book sees flame break out from his home, and Turnus in the twelfth sees fire break out from the tower on the city wall. But in none of these instances and many like them is there reason to see any cause at work beyond the normal tendency of the imagination to repeat itself, or to expect a significant relationship between the pairs.

Echoes of other kinds may be equally fortuitous. Thus, phrases such as *res rapuisse* or *legitque virum vir* have precise technical meanings in Roman life apart from the literal meanings in which Virgil applies them in his poem; but these technical meanings do not colour the value of them in their Virgilian contexts.[10] The doves that guide Aeneas to the Golden Bough have no doubt been suggested to Virgil's imagination by the foundation legend of the town of Cumae, in which the Chalcidic settlers of Cumae were guided by a dove to their destination;[11] for the Cumaean setting of the scene in the *Aeneid* coupled with the distinctive role of the doves makes this a reasonably certain inference. But recollection of this will not enrich the episode of the Golden Bough, because it has no useful relevance to it. Nor again is anything added to the story of the tame hind petted and garlanded by the Latin herdsman's daughter in the seventh book by the memory of the hind petted and garlanded by Sertorius in Roman history.* Yet the motif is curious enough for us to feel sure that it was from that celebrated story that the poet took his idea.

While therefore it is clear that some of the echoes and repetitions in the *Aeneid* have been sought by the poet with the intention that they should be felt as such, this is by no means so with all of them. Many have occurred simply because a thought or a phrase rose from the poet's memory as apt to his immediate need; and even if he was aware at the time of the original context, that context may still have no relevance to the new one. With Virgil, the creative act consists very largely in the re-fashioning and re-ordering of old materials in new combinations, and they may either retain or lose their former associations in the process. It follows that even in an unmistakable echo one must not assume significant associations, unless there are positive reasons for supposing that these are present.

Conversely, where an apparent echo affords evident and strongly significant associations one need not refuse to accept these for oneself because no proof exists that they were present in the poet's mind. For instance, it is fairly certain that the thought of Pompey's end

* Sertorius was a Roman officer who in the early years of the first century B.C. established for a time an independent government of his own in Spain. The story of the hind is told in Plutarch's *Life* of him, Chapter 11.

came into Virgil's mind as he described the death of Priam, because the striking similarities in the picture are reinforced by the strangeness in this context of the word meaning 'on the shore'.[12] But even if this were not so, the memory of Pompey and of Plutarch's account of his murder would still enrich the Virgilian passage for many readers and add reality and pathos to it. Or again, the words of Turnus as he reaches his decision—'have mercy on me, o powers of the world below, since the powers of this world are turned against me . . . I will go down to death unstained by that offence and worthy still of my great ancestors'—may well recall for some readers the similar phrases in Plutarch's account (in his *Life of Antony*) of the last hours of Cleopatra: 'if the gods below can or will help us, since those above have abandoned us . . .', and 'it was well done indeed, and as became the descendant of so many kings';[13] and though this apparent echo of another tragic catastrophe, still recent when Virgil wrote, may be fortuitous, and is anyway not likely to have been consciously intended, its associations harmonize with the spirit of the Virgilian passage and need not be repulsed. Similarly, we cannot know whether Virgil had in mind the epigram of Plato on the young man, 'bright once as morning star among the living and now as evening star among the dead', when he made the splendid simile in which the young hero Pallas has the beauty of the morning star in the eye of the onlookers as he sets out for the war in which he is to die.[14] But the prophetic relevance of the epigram is inevitably there for the reader who recalls it, whether Virgil intended this or not.

Nor again are we to shun as irrelevant associations evoked in a reading of the *Aeneid* which cannot possibly have been present consciously or sub-consciously to the poet because they could not be within the range of his direct experience, the meaning given to a phrase by the reader's own experience or by its recorded influence on the lives of other men, the symbolic value added to an episode by the symbolic role of something similar in later literature. To reject these as irrelevant because fortuitous would be to reject a distinctive virtue of Virgil's poetry. And indeed to regard them all as simply fortuitous would be mistaken; for though some such effects will be fortuitous in the full sense, some will reflect a universal quality in the poet's sensibility, and some will owe their later associations precisely to the echoing of Virgil's poem in the minds of later men. But in all this it is necessary in speaking of Virgil, whatever we may do in reading him, to draw some distinction between what we seem to hear as we listen to him and what we can suppose him actually to be saying.

There is thus much that can justly be understood to be allusive or symbolic in the *Aeneid*. But this, though important, is incidental to its essential character. In essence it is a story consisting of splendid and moving episodes, organized in a strongly shaped architectural pattern, and told in language of great expressive and emotive power. This story is centred on examples of intense and important human experience, tragedy and vocation. And this experience is not seen in isolation, but in a theological and a historical context. The humans act and suffer in a world governed by laws and powers that are over-whelmingly stronger than they, and that these laws and powers are by human standards morally imperfect enhances the tragic quality of the human experience. The human action and suffering is more-over part of a process leading to an end in history which is felt to matter more than the fortunes of the individual humans, yet so as to enhance rather than diminish their value. This end and object of the story is Rome, as the poet contemplates her greatness, and the peace among nations over which she presides, with the heightened emo-tions of a unique historical moment.

The idea of Rome is thus the dominant value in the Aeneid and the primary motive of its action; and many readers both in the ancient and in the modern world have been willing enough to accept this, and to find in the poem an expression not only of a man's feeling for his country, but also of the high role Rome has indeed had in history as an organizing and harmonizing and humanizing agency. It was after all only a generation after Virgil that the seeds of western christendom were spread in the ground prepared by the Roman peace by a Greek-speaking Jew from Asia Minor who was, like Virgil, a Roman citizen. But in a world no longer sympathetic to empires some may prefer to reflect that the motive of a poem is only one of its constituents, and not always the most important. The success of *Paradise Lost* as a poem, for instance, does not depend on whether Milton has had success in his avowed intention of justifying the ways of God to man. And so with the *Aeneid*, those who cannot enter with sympathy into Virgil's conception of Rome may find the meaning of his poem for themselves in its complementary theme, the impact of world forces and world movements on the lives of in-dividuals and the human qualities displayed in their response.

APPENDIX 1

The Text. Macrobius and Servius.
Donatus' Life of the poet

VIRGIL died in 19 B.C., and the *Aeneid* was prepared for publication
after his death by his friend and literary executor the poet Varius.
Our own text of the *Aeneid* is based chiefly on the evidence of two
manuscripts (P and M) of the fourth or fifth centuries A.D. and one
(R) which is believed to be of the fifth, none wholly complete but
all nearly so and supplementing one another's deficiencies. Portions
of the poem are also covered by manuscript fragments of the fourth
century or earlier. Moreover, a literary dialogue written at the turn
of the fourth and fifth centuries (the *Saturnalia* of Macrobius) includes numerous citations from Virgil's works; and, more important,
there has survived a full commentary on them (that of Servius)
composed at about the same date, the notes of which usually disclose
the text to which they refer and in a number of cases cite and discuss
variants. It will be seen from this that we have a good range of
information available about the state of the text of the *Aeneid* current
in the last hundred and fifty years of the western Roman empire—
the period running from, say, the Council of Nicaea in A.D. 325 to
the abdication of the last emperor in 475; and this information is
reinforced by the evidence of a number of manuscripts of the ninth
century which, in so far as they are not descendants of the manuscripts mentioned above, afford a separate witness through their own
ancestry to the range of variants possibly current in the fourth and
fifth centuries. The period thus indicated was separated from the
first appearance of the *Aeneid* by a time-space not much exceeding
that which separates ourselves from the age of Spenser and Shake-
speare. There is the difference of course that the text of Virgil was
distributed and reproduced, not by the stable medium of print, but
through manuscript copying with all its attendant risks of the in-
trusion and propagation of error. But in fact the text of the *Aeneid* as
it stood four hundred years after Virgil's death can be seen to have
exhibited relatively few variations other than those due to obvious
and explicable mistakes in particular manuscripts. This is no doubt
due in part to the fact that copies of good quality were at all times

available as a stabilizing influence in public libraries and elsewhere.[1] Of the significant variants which occur some may go back to alternatives or obscurities in the poet's own manuscript. But, as has been said already, the number of such variants is not great, though some of them are important.

The literary dialogue mentioned above, the *Saturnalia* of Macrobius, is supposed to represent the conversation at a dinner-party held at the holiday season which gives the work its name. The host is Vettius Agorius Praetextatus, a pious and cultivated nobleman and a great upholder of Roman traditions and in particular of the religious practices of Roman paganism; it happens that the epitaph of Praetextatus and his wife Paulina has survived (separately) and throws a touching and not unpleasing light upon this aspect of his character.[2] Chief among the participants is Quintus Aurelius Symmachus, another member of the Roman aristocracy and upholder of the old culture and the old religion; he has left behind him among other literary remains an eloquent appeal to the then emperor for the restoration to the senate-house of the statue and altar of Victory, installed there by Augustus, which had been removed, at the instance of the adherents of Christianity, a few years before the imagined date of this dialogue. Also among those present is a boorish and assertive person named Evangelus, presumably meant to be identified from his name as a Christian. And another guest is a certain Servius, said to be a professor engaged at that time in expounding the works of Virgil to classes of students at Rome. This is the author of the commentary which bears his name; but it appears from the introduction to the dialogue that Macrobius has taken a liberty with chronology in including him, and that his career did not begin in the lifetime of Praetextatus, who died in A.D. 385. The parts of the dialogue concerned with Virgil are Books 3 (ch. 1–12), 4, 5 and 6, and they deal successively with his alleged familiarity with various details of old Roman religious practice, with his use of rhetorical artifices, and with the echoes in his poetry of earlier poets, first of Homer and other Greeks and next of Ennius and other Latins. This literary material is no doubt largely compiled from earlier compilations rather than extracted from the author's memory of his own reading of the poets quoted. But the book affords a convenient means of obtaining an impression of the abundance and variety of this kind of literary echoes in Virgil's language. It has also a certain pathos of its own, as record of the attitudes and interests of an old culture already threatened with submersion.

The commentary of Servius is so named in the manuscripts which preserve it, and is thus associated with the commentator on Virgil who appears in Macrobius' dialogue and whose activity is dated by that dialogue to the turn of the fourth and the fifth century A.D. It is a full commentary and covers much the same range of matters as do the commentaries of modern scholars familiar to ourselves. It draws attention to the literary merits, real or supposed, of particular phrases or passages. It explains the meaning of words which are unusual or unusually applied, the way in which a sentence is to be construed, the relation of a sentence to its context. It notes peculiarities of grammar, explains proper names, provides etymologies, quotes phrases from earlier poets whom the poet is echoing, gives information about mythology, antiquities, historical sources, and so on. It preserves in this way a large mass of information accumulated by earlier students of philology and antiquities which we should not otherwise possess, including many fragments of early Latin poetry. On the other hand, it is in many ways a disappointing document. Its interpretations are often perverse or far-fetched, its information downright wrong or presented in a misleading manner. Thus in Helenus' words to Anchises (3.480) *o felix nati pietate* the commentator detects an allusion to Anchises' impending death. He takes *finem dedit ore loquendi* (6.76) as meaning that Aeneas prescribed to the Sibyl that she should give her response orally instead of writing it on leaves, though Virgilian usage shows that it means simply that he ceased speaking. He explains *ingentem sese clamore ferebat* (9.597) with the remark that the warrior described was not really huge but kept shouting that he was; though Virgilian usage and common sense agree that it means that he strode shouting defiance, a huge figure. The Sabine town Mutusca (7.711), because also called Trebula Mutusca, is identified with the river Trebia in northern Italy where Hannibal inflicted their first great defeat on the Romans in the second Punic war. The line 5.591 (*qua signa sequendi*) *frangeret indeprensus et inremeabilis error* is said to be 'a verse from Catullus', when the Catullan verse which it echoes really runs (Cat. 64.115) (*ne . . . egredientem*) *tecti frustraretur inobservabilis error*; and similarly the fourth book with its story of Dido's love and death is said to be 'taken in its entirety' from the third book of Apollonius' *Argonautica*, when the dependence is really much more limited. These examples are not untypical. It will be seen from them that the Servian commentary, though composed by and for people whose native language was Latin and who lived within a few centuries of Virgil himself, is of limited value as a guide to the understanding of the poem. It is however of great value as a source of earlier learning which would else have been lost to us, and of citations from poets whose works have not survived.

In certain manuscripts the material of the Servian commentary is found embedded verbatim in a longer commentary, to which the name of Servius is not attached. The non-Servian material in this is of the same general character as the Servian, but has also certain distinctive and uniform characteristics of its own. The resulting total thus appears to be a product of the conflation of two separate sets of material, both compiled in broadly the same period, that is to say the last hundred and fifty years of the western empire. This expanded commentary is conventionally known as *Servius Auctus*, or as *Servius Danielis*, after the French scholar who first published it at the end of the sixteenth century.

Prefixed to the commentary of Servius is a *Life* of Virgil; and several other ancient Lives of Virgil have been preserved. Of these the longest, the earliest and the most useful is that generally attributed to Aelius Donatus, a well-known grammarian of the fourth century A.D. and a teacher of St. Jerome. A translation of this Life is appended below. Circumstantial evidence (set out in the admirable introduction to the Oxford text of the *Lives*) makes it reasonably certain that the attribution to Aelius Donatus is correct, and also makes it reasonably certain that Donatus extracted most of his material verbatim from a *Life* of Virgil, now lost, by Suetonius, the author of the *Lives of the Caesars* and also of a series of monographs on famous men of learning and of letters. Suetonius wrote in the early years of the second century A.D., and thus within a century and a half of Virgil's death, not further removed from him than our day is from that of Keats and Shelley. Attempts have been made to distinguish by stylistic analysis the Suetonian and the non-Suetonian material in the *Life* attributed to Donatus, and certain passages deemed on this evidence to be non-Suetonian are bracketed in the translation of the *Life* which is printed below. It must not however be assumed that all that is not so bracketed is certainly Suetonian; nor, of course, that all that is Suetonian is necessarily true. It is clear that Suetonius preserved authentic information from people who knew Virgil well;[3] but it is clear also that already by his time this had become contaminated with a great amount of gossip and fable, especially concerning the poet's infancy and early years.

AELIUS DONATUS' *LIFE* OF VIRGIL

'Publius Vergilius Maro was a native of Mantua. His parents were of quite humble station, especially his father, who according to some accounts was a potter by trade, but most say that he was servant to a certain Magius, a minor official, and did well and married his master's daughter, [and increased his fortune substantially by buying woodland and bee-farming].

The poet was born in the first consulship of Cn. Pompeius and M. Licinius Crassus, on 15 October, in the village called Andes, not far from Mantua. His mother during her pregnancy dreamed that she had given birth to a branch of bay [which on touching the ground took root and immediately grew into a full-sized tree, covered with all manner of berries and blossoms]. The following day when she was going with her husband to visit a neighbouring farm she was obliged to turn off the road, and gave birth to her child in a ditch by the roadside. They say that the baby did not cry after its birth and had so gentle an expression that its parents felt sure already that their child's future would be a happy one. [And there occurred also another prophetic sign, in that a poplar shoot planted on the spot, according to local custom at the birth of a child, grew so quickly to be a tree that it equalled the growth of poplars planted long before. This tree was called for this reason Virgil's Tree, and was regarded as holy and was treated with great veneration by pregnant women and young mothers, who used to make and pay their vows at it.]

Virgil passed the first years of his life at Cremona, until he assumed the *toga* of manhood [which he did in his seventeenth year, in the second consulship of the same pair in whose first consulship he had been born; and it happened that on the very same day the poet Lucretius died]. About that time he moved from Cremona to Milan and thence shortly afterwards to Rome.

He was well built and tall, with a dark complexion and the appearance of a countryman. His health was variable; from time to time he suffered in his throat and stomach, and from headaches, and he often threw up blood. He ate and drank sparingly. He was somewhat inclined to pederasty [his particular favourites being Cebes and Alexander, whom he calls Alexis in the second *Eclogue*. Alexander was given to him by Asinius Pollio. Both of them were well-educated, and Cebes wrote poetry himself]. It has been widely asserted that Virgil also had a relationship with Plotia Hieria. But

Asconius Pedianus affirms that Plotia herself in her old age used to declare that Varius had indeed offered to share her with Virgil but that Virgil had persistently declined. In all other respects his conduct and demeanour were so respectable that at Naples he was commonly called Parthenias (i.e. 'Virginia'); and at Rome (where he rarely went), if ever he was recognized in public, he used to take refuge in the nearest house to escape being followed and pointed at. On one occasion he was offered the property of an exile by Augustus and refused to accept it. His own estate was worth about ten million sesterces, and came from the gifts of various friends. He had a house on the Esquiline, adjoining the Gardens of Maecenas, though he spent most of his time in Campania or Sicily, where he could get away from people.

He reached manhood before losing his parents, his father blind at the end of his life. [His brother Silo died when still a boy, and his brother Flaccus as a young man: it is Flaccus' death that Virgil laments in the person of Daphnis. He studied various subjects, among them medicine and, especially, mathematics (?).] He pleaded once in court, and never again; for according to Melissus he was slow of speech, almost like an illiterate.

His first essay in poetry was made in boyhood [a two-line epigram on a certain Ballista, keeper of a school of gladiators (?), who was stoned to death for his notorious highway robberies:

> Beneath this mound of stones Ballista lies buried;
> Now, traveller, by night or day go safely on your way.]

Next he wrote the *Catalepton*, and the *Priapea*, and the *Epigrammata*, and the *Dirae*: also the *Ciris*, and the *Culex* [when he was . . . years old, the subject of which is as follows. A shepherd was tired in the heat of the day; he had fallen asleep under a tree, and a snake was creeping towards him, when a mosquito from a near by pond came flying and bit him on the forehead. At once he squashed the mosquito, and killed the snake; and then put up a gravestone for the mosquito with the inscription

> Little mosquito, the guardian of the flock
> pays you this honour in death, as you deserve,
> for having saved his life.]

He also wrote the *Aetna*, though not all agree about his authorship of this. After this, he attempted a poem on Roman history, but found the subject uncongenial, and turned to pastoral poetry in his *Bucolics*; with the object especially of honouring Asinius Pollio and Alfenus Varus and Cornelius Gallus, because they had exempted him from loss in the distribution of lands beyond the Po which were being divided among the soldiers by order of the triumvirs after their victory at Philippi. Next he wrote the *Georgics* in honour of Maecenas, who (though then only slightly acquainted with him) had protected him against the violence of an ex-soldier who came near to killing him in a dispute about a piece of land. Finally he began the *Aeneid*, a story rich in incident and variety, and a counterpart, as it were, of both *Iliad* and *Odyssey* together; one moreover in which both Greek and Roman places and characters were involved together, and which was designed (this being his special intention) to embrace an account of the origins both of Rome and of Augustus.

It is recorded that when he was writing the *Georgics* he used each day early to dictate a considerable number of lines which he had composed and then spend the whole day working them over and reducing them to a very few; he said well that he produced his poetry as a she-bear does her cubs, licking it gradually into shape. The *Aeneid* he sketched out first in prose and divided into twelve books, and then set to turning it into a poem piece by piece, as the fancy took him, not following any set order in the process. Moreover, to avoid checking the flow of his invention, he left some passages unfinished, and in others inserted trivial verses to sustain the narrative temporarily, which he humorously used to say were to serve as 'props' to hold up the fabric of his work until the permanent supports should come to take their place.

The *Bucolics* he completed in three years, the *Georgics* in seven, and the *Aeneid* in eleven. The *Bucolics* on their publication met with immediate success, so much so that they used often to be recited on the stage by singers. The *Georgics* he read aloud to Augustus, on four consecutive days, on the emperor's way back to Rome after the victory at Actium, while he was resting at Atella to recover from an affection of the throat. Maecenas on this occasion took over the task of reading when Virgil's voice failed him and obliged him to stop. Virgil recited poetry in a most melodious voice and with an art that lent his recitation extraordinary charm. Indeed, Seneca has recorded that the poet Julius Montanus used to say that he would steal some phrases from Virgil "if only he could steal his voice and delivery too; for the same verses that sounded admirable when he spoke them seemed empty and flat without him".

The *Aeneid* when hardly begun aroused such expectancy that Sextus Propertius was not afraid to declare

> Give way you poets of Rome, and you of Greece;
> a greater work than the *Iliad* is in the making.

And Augustus, when he was away on his campaign against the Cantabriges, wrote begging the poet, in terms which mixed entreaty with good-natured menace, to send him (in Augustus' own words) "either the preliminary outline, or any specimen passage" that he liked. But it was only long afterwards, when the poem was substantially complete, that Virgil would recite any of it to the emperor, and then three books only, the second, fourth and sixth—the last of these to the great distress of Octavia, who being present at the recitation is said to have fainted at the words referring to her son *tu Marcellus eris . . .*, and was only with difficulty revived. He also recited to larger companies, but not often, and then usually the passages about which he was in doubt, in order to find out the verdict of others' taste. We are told that Eros his freedman and secretary used in his old age to tell how Virgil once in the course of a recitation completed impromptu two unfinished lines. For having in his text *Misenum Aeoliden . . .*, he added *quo non praestantior alter . . .*, and again after *aere ciere viros . . .* in a similar fit of inspiration he added *Martemque accendere cantu*; and immediately thereupon told Eros to write both these additions into his text.

In his fifty-second year, intending to give the *Aeneid* its final finish, he planned to go abroad into retirement in Greece and Asia and for three whole years to devote himself wholly to revision, so as to be able to pass the rest of his life in the study of philosophy. But having near the outset of his journey met Augustus at Athens on his way back to Rome from Greece, and resolving to stay with him and accompany him back to Rome, he went on a sight-seeing visit to the nearby town of Megara, on a very hot day. He fell ill; but he persisted in taking ship for Italy none the less, and his condition worsened and was already grave when he reached Brundisium. There he died a few days later, on 21 September, in the consulship of Cn. Sentius and Q. Lucretius. His remains were taken to Naples and there laid to rest in the tomb which now stands on the road to Puteoli, just short of the second milestone [on which is the following two-line epigram of his own composition

> Mantua was my birthplace. In Calabria I died, before my time.
> I rest at Naples. I sang of pastures, farms and heroes.]

He left half his estate to Valerius Proculus, his half-brother by another father, and a quarter to Augustus, and a twelfth to Maecenas, with the residue to L. Varius and Plotius Tucca [who afterwards edited the *Aeneid* by the emperor's command. On this subject there are the following verses by Sulpicius of Carthage.

> Virgil had ordered to be devoured by flames this poem
> in which is told the story of the Phrygian prince.
> Tucca and Varius refuse, and you, o Caesar, forbid
> that it be done, careful for the honour of Roman history.
> Ill-fated Pergamum came near to falling twice by fire,
> and Troy was threatened with a second burning.]

Virgil, before he left Italy, had tried to get Varius to agree to burn the *Aeneid* if anything should happen to himself, but Varius had firmly refused to give such a promise. Accordingly, the poet in his last illness asked repeatedly for the box containing his manuscript, intending to burn the poem with his own hands. But no one would bring it to him, and he gave no specific direction about it. In his will he bequeathed his writings to this same Varius and to Tucca, on the condition that they should not publish anything which he would not have published himself (*or*, which he had not published himself). In the event, Varius published the poem, on Augustus' instruction, with very little editing, as can be seen from the fact that he left the unfinished verses as they stand. Many people since then have tried to complete them, but with little success [because of the difficulty that really all Virgil's half-lines are complete in sense, except *quem tibi iam Troia*]. A professor of literature named Nisus used to say that he had heard from his elders that Varius changed the order of two books, moving the one which stood originally second to stand third in order; and further that he amended the beginning of the first book by removing the following verses

> I who once set my song to the music of a humble straw,
> and then forsook the woods and taught the neighbouring
> fields to obey the farmer's greediest demands—a boon
> for husbandmen—ah, now instead of Mars' grim . . .

Hostile critics of Virgil have never been lacking [and no wonder, for even Homer has had his detractors]. When the *Bucolics* first came out a certain Numitorius wrote some *Anti-Bucolics*, two pieces only [and those a vulgar parody], of which the first begins thus

> Tityrus, if you have a warm cloak, what need to shelter
> under your beech-tree?

and the second thus (?)

> Tell me Damoetas, whose herd are these? Is that Latin?
> No; it's Aegon's; our people speak this way in the country.

Another person, when Virgil was reciting the passage of the *Georgics* which contains the line

> Take off your coat to plough, and likewise to sow

interpolated

> . . . and you'll soon catch cold and get a fever.

There is also a book against the *Aeneid* by Carvilius Pictor, with the title *Aeneidomastix*. M. Vipsanius used to speak of Virgil as inventor with the encouragement of Maecenas, of a new kind of artificiality, neither extravagant nor affectedly simple, but based on common words and for that reason not at once perceived. Herennius has catalogued Virgil's faults, Perellius Faustus his borrowings as well. Again, there are the eight volumes of Q. Octavius Avitus' '*Similarities*', showing what verses Virgil has derived from other writers and from where. Asconius Pedianus in the book which he wrote against the detractors of Virgil cites only a few complaints against him, and those mostly relating to matters of fact or to his borrowings from Homer, and says that Virgil used to rebut the charge of plagiarizing Homer with the following remark: "Only let such critics try to do the same themselves. They would soon find that it is easier to steal his club from Hercules than to steal a line from Homer". Nevertheless (says Asconius) he had planned to retire abroad and pare and prune the whole work until even his hostile critics were satisfied.'

Such is the best of the ancient *Lives* of Virgil. It contains evidently a large admixture of nonsense, or romance. Nevertheless, most of the statements in it which bear on the composition of the *Aeneid* seem to be confirmed by facts observable in the poem itself—facts moreover which are not so obvious that the statements in the *Life* could be supposed, with any plausibility, to have been invented to explain them.

APPENDIX 2

On two passages said to have been excised by the first editors of the poem

Lines 1.1a–1d

A STORY is preserved in the Donatan and Servian *Lives* of Virgil (see pp. 114 ff. above) that the *Aeneid* as the poet left it did not begin with the familiar 'Arms I sing and a man, who . . .', but with four lines preceding and leading into this, and running as follows: 'I am he who (*or* I who) once set my song to the music of a humble straw, and then forsook the woods and taught the neighbouring fields to obey the farmer's greediest demands—a boon for husbandmen: but now (*or* -ah, now instead) of Mars' grim (arms I sing . . . etc.).¹ The story affirms that these four lines were excised by Virgil's literary executors when they prepared the poem for publication. They appear in none of the manuscripts which have come down to us from the ancient world, and it is clear that the opening now familiar has always been canonical. Thus while Ovid refers to Lucretius' *De Rerum Natura* by its opening words as 'the *Aeneadum genetrix*', Martial refers similarly to the *Aeneid* as 'the *Arma virum*'.²

The *Life* by Servius states it as a fact that Virgil began his poem with the four lines quoted. But comparison with the *Life* by Donatus, an earlier work, shows how much caution is required in the face of such positive statements by Servius, for it specifies the source of the story. According to the Donatan *Life*—'a professor of literature named Nisus used to say (p. 119 above) that he had heard (? as a young man) from his elders that Varius (Virgil's literary executor) changed the order of two books (at the beginning of the poem: the text of the *Life* is confused here and the particulars uncertain); and further that he amended the beginning of the first book by removing the following verses . . .'. It will be seen from this that the story, so far from recording an established fact, is founded on a piece of hearsay. It will be seen also that the source which reports it is manifestly untrustworthy; for the order of the books as it now stands is plainly not the work of anyone but the poet, and could not have been produced from an originally different order without a process of major surgery. It is of course quite possible that by some oversight a book or books had been wrongly numbered or misplaced among the poet's papers, but that is not what the story pretends.

Intrinsically the tale that the *Aeneid* was meant to begin with these prefatory verses is exceedingly improbable. Virgil did indeed append some lines about himself—celebrated and admirable lines— at the end of his *Georgics*, and Statius later did the same at the end of his epic the *Thebaid*. But these concluding addresses to the reader do not intrude on the poems themselves, which have already been completed; they are like the artist's signature on a work of art. The beginning is a different matter. It is quite conceivable that an epic poet might refer to himself at the beginning of his work in an in- vocation, a prayer for inspiration of the like. But it is hard to credit that he would begin it with a piece of trivial biography, irrelevant to all that follows and yet woven on to the syntax of the opening sentence of the narrative itself. Certainly Virgil's Greek predecessors Homer and Apollonius had not done so; nor were any of the Latins who followed him to do so, Lucan, Statius, Valerius Flaccus, Silius Italicus. It is perhaps worth noting here that the received and familiar opening of the *Aeneid* not only states the subject, in the usual epic manner, but also includes echoes of the great epics of which Virgil was most conscious in making his own. The first two lines echo the rhythm of the beginning of the *Iliad*: *arma virumque cano . . . /Italiam . . .* corresponds to μῆνιν ἄειδε θεὰ . . . /οὐλομένην. The first line echoes the thought of the beginning of the *Odyssey*: 'a man, who . . .'. And the phrase *arma virumque* itself is very likely an aural echo of a word-group recurrent in Ennius' *Annales* (with various meanings); for *arma virum* (with different meaning) occurs soon afterwards in the first book itself, while in the ninth book are three similar groups, *arma viros*, *in arma viros*, *sinite arma viris*, amid a number of observably Ennian echoes.[3] If these reminiscences of the poem's literary antecedents have a value in the opening of the *Aeneid*, this would be lost if something else were put before them.

Supposing that the story about these four lines is not true, it remains to offer an explanation of how it could arise, and where the lines come from. One possibility is that the lines are indeed Virgil's own, but that they were never meant to be part of the *Aeneid* and were thus never excised from it by the editors. It is possible (for anyone who does not think the style of these lines un-Virgilian) to imagine the poet amusing himself with such a fancy, even in the margin of his manuscript, without for a moment intending his fancy to be part of his poem. If the existence of the verses became known, the story of excision by the editors would be a natural consequence. But a more sophisticated explanation has been suggested, and it is as follows.[4] In Martial's ninth book there is talk in the introduction of a bust of the poet which a friend of his, an amateur of letters, is installing in his library. Martial has been asked to provide an epigram to be inscribed under the bust as title, and this he does. The epigram begins '*ille ego* . . .', like the first of the four lines in which Virgil is supposed to refer to himself. Again, the numerous articles described in short epigrams in Martial's fourteenth book include 'a parchment Virgil', of which it is said that 'the first page bears a portrait of the poet himself'.[5] From this it is easy to conceive that an early edition de luxe of the *Aeneid* might have a picture of the poet adjoining the first page of the text, with a title under it in verse so constructed as to construe grammatically with the beginning of the text itself. This title of course might be composed by anyone, and without any intention to pass it off as Virgil's work. But presently it could well happen that someone propounded the theory that it was the real original beginning of the *Aeneid* and had been 'removed' by the editors.

THE HELEN EPISODE
Lines 2.567–588

In the second book of the *Aeneid* the disappearance of Aeneas' companions (line 566) leaves him, after witnessing the death of Priam, alone on the roof of the royal palace. He is standing there when (589) his mother Venus appears to him and warns him to control his anger and think of his family: the gods are determined on the destruction of Troy. In between the lines mentioned there stands in most modern texts a passage (567–88) of twenty-two lines in which Aeneas is described as seeing Helen, as she tries to conceal herself, and thinking to kill her in revenge for all the misery she has caused. This passage does not appear in any of the MSS that have come down to us from the ancient world and evidently was not in the text of Virgil then current. It is preserved in the enlarged version of the Servian Commentary (p. 114 above) and is referred to in the Servian *Life* of Virgil, where the author says that the lines are by Virgil and are 'known to have been excised', presumably by the poet's literary executors who have been mentioned just before.

As we know from the case of the four lines alleged to have been

removed from the beginning of the poem, no reliance can be placed
on Servius' statement about the history of this passage. Our view of
its origin and history will have to be governed by other considerations.

It must be said to begin with that if the passage is not included it
leaves the narrative at that point incoherent. There are three reasons
for this conclusion, and one of them at least is inescapable. First, the
construction, if the passage is omitted, runs (565–6 and 589–90): 'my
comrades all left me, leaping down to the ground or throwing themselves in despair into the flames; when my mother appeared to me,
plain to see . . .'. It is possible here to understand 'when' as 'whereupon', but it is awkward. Secondly, Venus after reminding Aeneas of
his family continues: 'it is not the baleful beauty of Helen or the
fault of Paris that is cause of Troy's overthrow, it is the merciless
anger of the gods'. It is perhaps not inevitable that the reference to
Helen and Paris should have a motive in the immediate context,
but one would expect it to have, and if 567–88 are absent it has not.
Thirdly, in line 562 Aeneas is thinking of his family; and in lines
596 ff Venus tells him with an air of reproach to do precisely that:
'will you not before all else see in what state you have left your
father, feeble as he is from age, and whether your wife and son still
live?' This is an impossible sequence, without some passage intervening in which Aeneas' thoughts are being (as they are in 567–88)
distracted elsewhere. Thus it is clear that without 567–88 the text is
incoherent. It is clear too that when those lines are present all the
difficulties recited disappear. Instead of the awkward sequence of
565–6 and 589 there results the easy and natural sequence of 588 and
589: 'thus was I raging, thus exclaiming, when lo my mother
appeared, plain to see . . .'. Further Venus' reference to Helen and
Paris as not the real cause of Troy's undoing has its cue in Aeneas'
thoughts of vengeance on Helen. Finally, when Venus tells Aeneas to
think before all else of his family, this rebukes him for having let his
thoughts of vengeance expel them from his mind. It is clear that there
is a gap in the narrative without these lines, and that these lines have
been composed to fill it. And they do in fact fill it with very good
effect. A puzzle seems at first reading to arise because in line 570
Helen is said to be noticed by Aeneas *erranti passimque oculos per
cuncta ferenti*, and this, if *erranti* bore its commonest meaning here,
would mean that Aeneas was roaming the city, whereas both before
(566) and later (632) he is still on the roof of Priam's palace. But
erranti need not mean 'as I roamed': it can equally well mean 'as I

hesitated', and evidently does have that meaning here.[6] There is thus no discrepancy between the passage 567–88 and the immediate context in which Servius says it was meant to stand.

It does however exhibit some peculiarities that call for comment. To begin with there are seven instances within seventeen lines of a distinctive metrical effect (not itself uncommon in Virgil) whereby the stressed syllable of the third foot is a monosyllabic word preceded by elision: e.g. *et poenas Danaum et deserti coniugis iras*. This exceptional frequency might surprise in a finished Virgilian passage, but need not surprise if this passage, an emotional one anyway, is an early draft that still awaits re-working. Again, the transferred epithet in *sceleratas sumere poenas* (576) is remarkable, but not more remarkable than many Virgilian liberties with language; for instance *quod scelus . . . merente?* (7.307) for *cuius sceleris poenam merente?* Linguistically there is nothing in the passage to make Virgilian authorship seem unlikely.[7] What might at first sight excite more suspicion is a gross contradiction of fact between what is said of Helen here, where she is described as hiding from the Greeks in fear at the taking of Troy, and what is said in Book 6, where Deiphobus tells of her assisting them and leading them on. But this discrepancy is not in fact at all incompatible with Virgilian authorship of the passage, for other discrepancies exist between different parts of the poem: for instance between the two accounts of Palinurus' end in Book 5 and in Book 6. They seem to result from a habit of concentrating the imagination on the passage in hand, and are not surprising in a poem of large dimensions, full of varied episodes, and composed (as Donatus' *Life* says) *particulatim*. They would have been removed, if obtrusive, in the final revision which the poet did not live to complete.

There is thus nothing about the passage itself which need make one doubt that it is Virgil's work.[8] It could have stood in his manuscript with an indication that it needed re-working, because of the contradiction with Book 6 or for other reasons; and in that case it would be natural for the editors to omit it from the published poem. Servius' story that the passage was excised by the editors is thus intrinsically plausible, if we allow that excision may be an over-statement for non-inclusion.

It must still be remembered that we do not know Servius' authority for the text he transmits and his report about it, and that his own acceptance of them is no evidence of their authenticity. Nothing is said on the subject in the earlier *Life* by Donatus. This does not discredit the story, since Donatus can have reserved mention for the appropriate place in his commentary, which has not survived. On the other hand the silence of the Donatan *Life* does imply that the story of these lines, from wherever it is derived, is not derived from the hearsay of 'Nisus the professor', which Donatus specifies as origin of the legend about the four lines supposed to have been removed by Virgil's editors from the beginning of the poem.

A further consideration is this. If 2.567–588 are not by Virgil they are by an extremely expert imitator. Such an imitator must have known his Virgil extremely well. He could not therefore have fallen by accident (as the poet at one stage of the poem's composition could have) into the contradiction between what is said here and what is said in the no less striking passage in Book 6 about the conduct of Helen at the fall of Troy. If therefore the story given by Servius is wholly rejected, we must imagine a very sophisticated imitator who has introduced the contradiction on purpose, in order to pass off his handiwork under cover of some such story as that which Servius relates. This seems a less plausible theory than the simpler theory that the Servian story is in its essentials true.

But if the above reasoning inclines us to believe that these lines 2.567–88 are Virgil's work, we have still to remember that we do not know how they were preserved, though excluded from the published text of the poem, through the four centuries or more that elapsed before the first mention of them that has come down to us.[9]

APPENDIX 3

Evidence of the unrevised state of the poem. Internal discrepancies. Incomplete lines. Make-shift lines and phrases

DONATUS' *Life* of Virgil (pp. 114 ff. above), itself a work of the fourth century A.D. but based evidently on a *Life* by Suetonius composed at the turn of the first and second centuries, not much more than a hundred years after Virgil's death, affirms that the poet at the time of his death had in mind to spend three full years in revising and correcting the *Aeneid*, which was then in substance complete (*perfecta demum materia* is the term which the writer of the *Life* has used a little earlier).

This tradition, that the poem had still much work to be done on it when Virgil died, is proved true by the presence in it of a number of internal inconsistencies and other irregularities of a kind so evident that an author as careful as Virgil would have been certain to remove them before publishing his work. These are not important in the sense that their presence appreciably blemishes the poem, or puts in doubt the fact that it is 'in substance complete'. They are rather in the nature of occasional loose ends and rough edges.

In some cases of course it may be questioned whether what seems to oneself an irregularity would have seemed so to the poet, or have been noticed by him at all. Thus, the fact that the Trojans are said at 1.755 and again at 5.626 to be in the seventh summer of their wanderings, though a winter has passed (4.193 and 309) at Carthage between the two occasions, is a triviality that might in any case have escaped notice. When the sign of the Eaten Tables and the sign of the Sow with Thirty Young are received by the hero in Books 7 and 8 respectively, as assurance of his arrival in the promised land, it seems strange that there is no recall in either passage of the dramatic prophecies of these events delivered in Book 3 by the Harpy Celaeno and by Helenus; but such recall is not inevitable, and there is no positive contradiction in either case between the prophecy and the event. Book 10 ends with the death of Mezentius in single combat while the battle is at its height, and Book 11 begins with the dawning of the next day; no other transition between books in the poem is comparably abrupt, but that does not prove that Virgil could not have remained satisfied with this one.

But whatever one makes of cases such as these, there are some in which oversight, or lack of completion, seems the only possible explanation. Thus in Book 2 there is *either* a gap waiting to be filled between lines 566 and 589 *or* a passage which gives an account of Helen's behaviour on the night of the fall of Troy quite different from and irreconcilable with that which is given in Book 6. At the end of Book 2 Aeneas is told by Creusa's ghost (781–2) that his future home will be in Hesperia, by the side of the Tiber; but in the following Book 3 the Trojans are ignorant of their destination and only learn of it from the apparition of the Penates in Crete after a disastrous mistake in their choice of a place to settle. In Book 5 Palinurus falls overboard, overpowered by sleep, on the night before the arrival of the Trojans at Cumae, as the ships glide before a favourable breeze over a sea miraculously calmed for them by Neptune; but in the following Book 6 his ghost tells Aeneas, on the night after the arrival of the Trojans at Cumae, that he was swept for three nights across the sea in stormy weather as he clung to a piece of timber (349–56); and the stormy setting and the poet's remark that he was lost 'on the voyage from Africa' (338) suggest that at this point the narrator is thinking of the situation at the beginning of the previous book rather than that at the end in which, as the poem stands, Palinurus' misfortune actually takes place. Again, at the beginning of the adventure of Nisus and Euryalus in Book 9 the two young heroes are introduced with a description which makes it appear that the reader is not expected to know them (176 ff.), whereas in fact they have already figured prominently in the foot-race in the Games in Book 5. Finally, in the account in Book 10 of the arrival by sea of Aeneas and his relieving forces the time is night in 147–62 and night again (or still) at 216; but line 215 runs 'and now daylight had left the sky . . .', implying that day has intervened since 162, though no other indication of this has been given meanwhile. Irregularities such as these do not impair the poem's total effect, but they are enough to show that it had still to receive its final finish at the time of the poet's death.

METRICALLY INCOMPLETE LINES AND MAKESHIFT PHRASES

Since it seems clear that, as Donatus' *Life* of Virgil says, the *Aeneid* at the time of Virgil's death was still unfinished, in the sense of

lacking final revision, though in substance complete, it is natural to
ascribe to this circumstance the presence in the poem of between
fifty and sixty metrically incomplete lines. Examples of this metrical
anomaly occur in every book, but not in even distribution: thus
there are nine cases in Book 2, and six apiece in Books 7, 9 and 10,
but only two apiece in Books 6 and 11 and one in Book 12. The
length varies from one foot (e.g. 3.640 *rumpite*) to four feet (e.g.
9.721 *bellatorque animo deus incidit*). In a few cases (e.g. 4.361 *Italiam
non sponte sequor*) the rhythm of the phrase forming the incomplete
line is very effective; but this effect would not be diminished if the
following sentence began by completing the line instead of starting
a new one. In most cases no useful rhythmical effect appears to be
associated with the phenomenon; and the very uneven distribution
of its occurrence among the books of the poem seems to exclude the
possibility that it was sought as a deliberate variation to break the
long succession of regular hexameters in a poem of epic length. It is
therefore natural to suppose that Virgil would have revised his poem,
had he lived, to exclude incomplete lines, as did all other hexameter
poems before and after his. Moreover, if he had intended to retain
incomplete lines as a deliberate artistic device, this extraordinary
intention would surely have been remembered by his literary
executors or his secretary and have found its way into the tradition
about him preserved by grammarians and commentators; but in
fact no such idea is recorded as having occurred to anyone in the
ancient world, and the natural assumption seems to have been
general that the incomplete lines are there because the author had
not finished his work on the poem when he died.

This assumption presents no difficulty at all. For Virgil's treatment of the hexameter is distinguished from that of his predecessors
by his practice of ending his sentences and paragraphs at varying
positions within the line; while tradition reports that he composed
by dictation, in bursts, and would leave gaps or make do with
temporary expedients in order not to break the flow of his inspiration when he was in a creative mood. These circumstances would be
very likely to produce a state of the still unrevised poem which
should include a number of metrically incomplete lines, and those
especially of the types to which most of those found in the *Aeneid*
conform: namely, ends of paragraphs, and phrases introductory to
speeches (e.g. 8.469 *rex prior haec*:, 12.631 *Turnus ad haec*:).

There is thus no reason to see in the incomplete lines anything but
a consequence of the unrevised state of the poem and of Virgil's

method of composition. However, there is a singular fact that should be noted. Incomplete lines occur in every book of the poem, including those (2, 4 and 6) which Virgil is said to have read aloud to Augustus when the poem as a whole was 'in substance complete'. Unless therefore he worked further on these books after the recitation—assuming the story of this recitation to be true—it will follow that he did not regard the presence of incomplete lines as an obstacle to public exhibition of his work; and this is implied too in the story (also recorded in Donatus' *Life*) that he completed 6.164–5 on an inspiration which came to him in the very act of recitation, line 164 having till then consisted of the two words *Misenum Aeoliden*. This seems to indicate a readiness to exhibit the poem with incomplete lines still in it; but also a disposition to remove the anomaly which such lines constituted.

In speaking of Virgil's method of composition the *Life* says: 'to avoid halting the flow of his inspiration (*ne quid impetum moraretur*), he left some passages unfinished, and others again he filled in with quite trivial makeshift props, to serve until adequate construction could take their place'. This statement about the makeshifts is confirmed by the evidence of the text as we have it, in which occasionally phrases occur that are inappropriate to their context. For instance, Venus in her complaint to Jupiter (10.18 ff.) about the attack on the Trojan camp that has been made in Aeneas's absence exclaims (24): 'they are fighting even within the ramparts' bank, and the moat is swollen high with blood'. Here the concluding phrase is appropriate as part of a particular scene that is in mind. But when the same words recur in Turnus' retort to his critic Drances (11.382) 'loud words fly from you when all is safe, when the ramparts' bank holds off the enemy and the moat is not swollen high with blood', they are extravagant and so ineffective in their new context, and are evidently due to an aural reminiscence of the earlier passage stimulated by the reference to the 'ramparts' bank'. Again, when the god Apollo descends to warn the young Ascanius to be content with his feat of arms and not expose himself further (9.638 ff.), he is described as having assumed the appearance and all the attributes of an old man named Butes, once armour-bearer to Anchises and now attached by Aeneas as mentor to his son, and these attributes are specified as 'voice and features and the dreadful ring of arms'. Here the last phrase has no point in reference to the aged counsellor; perhaps it came into Virgil's mind from the description of Apollo in the first book of the *Iliad* which is echoed a few lines later in his account of the god's departure from the scene. One can feel reasonably sure that the process of final revision of the poem would have included the removal of awkwardnesses such as these—a completion in fact of the process described in the *Life* as habitual, in which a phase of rapid composition was followed by a phase of intensive rejection, selection and repair. The process of final revision was, according to the *Life*, to have occupied Virgil for three whole years.

APPENDIX 4

Some imperfections of execution and design

THERE are a number of imperfections in the *Aeneid* which are not merely signs of lack of finish. It is worth while reviewing some examples of these, not as an exercise in fault-finding, but because appreciation of a book is not helped by disguising its limitations. It may be of course that some of the weaknesses to be reviewed would have been removed in the final revision of the poem. We have no means of knowing.

One thing which is apt to trouble a modern reader cannot perhaps properly be described as a fault, but reflects a peculiarity of the conventions of Latin poetic diction. This is an occasionally extravagant use of metonymy and of hyperbole. Thus the Wooden Horse is variously described in Book 2 as made of fir (16), maple (112), oak (230) and pine (258); and a ship bound northwards may be said apparently (5.2) to sail on a north wind, or a ship bound southwards on a south wind (3.70). These are simply variants of the common type of metonymy whereby the term for a part is allowed to designate the whole, as 'keel' or 'poop' may stand for 'ship'; or the special for the general, as 'sand' may be said for 'earth', or 'Dorian' for 'Greek'. What the horse is made of is wood, and what bears the ships along is wind, and in the passages referred to there is no more to it than that. Again, in the matter of hyperbole, we may be prepared to accept that a shout 'strikes the stars' (2.488); but it is disturbing to most modern tastes when a stone thrown by a warrior of no remarkable distinction is described as 'no small part of a hill' (10.128). Similarly it seems an extravagance when Turnus (12.899) takes up and throws a stone 'which twelve men of our time would not easily carry'. And the idea that the leather strips which the boxer (5.404) binds about his hands and wrists consist of 'seven huge ox-hides' is not so much extravagant as grotesque.

In these cases the poet has carried perhaps too far a tendency generally present in the poetic diction of his time. In other cases he seems to allow his imagination to concentrate on a particular moment to the exclusion of its context, so that discrepancies are felt between the conception now governing the picture and that which prevailed earlier or will prevail a little later on. Thus the Sibyl tells Aeneas (6.146) that the Golden Bough will let itself be plucked without resistance if he is indeed the man chosen by destiny; but when the time comes it requires a tug (211) to pluck it. King Latinus' resistance to his people's clamour for war is described as immovable (7.586 ff.), in an impressive simile; but it is then *at once* added that he withdraws to his palace and yields up the reins of power. Sometimes this shift of conception seems to be due simply to inattention on the poet's part; sometimes it can be traced to a conflict between convention and reality or between rival conventions in his mind. Thus the young warrior Lausus is at one moment a frail and youthful figure and we hear of his *levia arma* and the tunic woven for him by his mother (10.818), and a moment later he is a Homeric hero of huge proportions *ingentem atque ingenti vulnere victum* (842). Evander wakes in his 'humble' dwelling (8.455), appropriate to the primitive simplicity of his rustic kingdom, but the dwelling a few lines later (461) has a 'lofty threshold', presumably because it is the home of an epic prince. Juturna has been made a nymph and immortal by Jupiter as compensation for having been deflowered by him (12.140), because this in one class of myths is a familiar explanation of the deification of mortal women; but the Jupiter of the *Aeneid*, author and upholder of the principle of order in the universe, is a quite different character from the Jupiter who is hero of this kind of tale.

These are details. But the same sort of discrepancy between the conceptions governing the poet's imagination at different moments can be observed in more important matters. In the fifth book the intended development of the story requires that Aeneas should experience a moment of discouragement, to give a cue for the dream in which Anchises comforts him and promises him a vision in the underworld of the future of his descendants. The attempted burning of the ships gives occasion for such a moment of discouragement. But it passes credibility that Aeneas should be so seriously discouraged as to think, as he is portrayed as doing, of abandoning his enterprise altogether, in the very last stage of it, and after he has uprooted himself from Carthage on account of it, and after his prayer for help has been answered by a miracle, because of the loss of four out of twenty of his ships in a friendly country where they could easily be replaced. Or again, the intended development of the story requires that Turnus be kept out of Aeneas' way after he has killed Pallas in the tenth book, so that the encounter of the rival heroes may be postponed to the end of the story; and the *Iliad* has suggested the expedient of having him lured from the scene by a phantom fashioned by a god. But the resulting situation in which the champion and commander-in-chief of the Latin-Rutulian forces has vanished from the field and turned up at his own home while the battle is at its height is one which the poet thereafter treats as non-existent. In both these cases the poet's concentration on the immediate situation seems to have led him to forget the requirements of the wider context. And this seems to have happened also in his account of Turnus' appearance at the making of the truce in the twelfth book (12.216 ff.). The intended development of the story requires the Latins to begin to regret the pact of single combat made between Turnus and Aeneas; and this has led the poet to describe Turnus in terms which make him a subdued, youthful and pathetic figure.[1] This is too sharply at variance with the image of Turnus created and maintained in all the rest of the poem: the seasoned warrior (7.474, 11.224), the hero of splendid stature, towering by a head among his fellows (7.783 ff.), who can hurl a missile of the kind shot by siege-engines (9.705) or throw a stone so big that twelve ordinary men would scarcely suffice to carry it (12.899); and more immediately it is at variance with the figure of the raging Turnus of the day before the duel (12.101 ff.) and his irresistible slaughterous progress later in the battle (12.326 ff.). It is admittedly the case of course that Aeneas is supposed to be an even more formidable figure, so that the match seems to the spectators uneven; and it is the case also that Turnus now sees Aeneas probably for the first time. But his appearance at the truce-making remains unharmonized with the character and attributes that he wears in the rest of the story. This conflict of concepts is incidentally illustrated by a detail that is otherwise unimportant: Turnus is armed with two light spears at the truce-making (12.165), though he is armed with a single big spear before and after (91 ff. and 711–12).

The conflict of divergent concepts in the poet's mind can be seen again in his description of the Latin people. He tells us at the outset (7.46) that Latinus' reign has been long and peaceful; but the Tiber god tells Aeneas (8.55) that the Latins are always at war with the people of Pallanteum. As the tribes of Italy assemble for the war, the poet says (7.623) that Ausonia has been till then undisturbed in peace; and Diomede warns the 'men of old Ausonia' not to break the peace they live in and stir up war of which they have no knowledge (8.253 ff.); but Jupiter has prophesied at the beginning of the poem that Aeneas will have to tame a wild and fiery people in Italy

(1.263), and Anchises has warned Aeneas that he will have to fight in Latium with a fierce and hardy breed of men (5.730), and the warrior Numanus shot down by Ascanius in the fighting for the camp boasts (9.602 ff.) that the men of Italy are a hardy race always engaged in war and rapine. It is conceivable that underlying this diversity of conceptions is a distinction between the Latins as peaceable and their neighbours the Rutulians as warlike (cf. for instance 7.426 where Allecto chides Turnus with his unrewarded services in enabling the Latins to enjoy peace under his protection, and Amata's argument at 7.367 ff. that the Rutulians are a 'foreign' people for the purposes of the oracles which require a foreign husband for Lavinia); but this distinction has not been preserved or developed, and two traditional conceptions of ancient Italy are left conflicting—the one of Italy as scene of the golden age of primitive peace and innocence, the other of Italy as mother of the tough and hardy and pugnacious qualities which when regulated by discipline produced the irresistible might of Roman arms. In this case the conflict is between two traditional concepts. A conflict of another kind, between the influence of a Homeric exemplar and the context in which its Virgilian counterpart is set, can be observed in the story of the sortie of Nisus and Euryalus in Book 9. In the Homeric Doloneia the lending of equipment to Ulysses and Diomede by the other chiefs is explained by the fact that they have risen from their beds to attend the council, but Nisus and Euryalus have been on guard and the repetition of the Homeric motif in their case (9.303 ff.) has no point. Again, Ulysses and Diomede have the normal Homeric hero's preoccupation with booty and with inflicting loss on the enemy, but the assignment for which Nisus and Euryalus have volunteered is to get a message through to their absent commander, and the slaughter they inflict on their sleeping enemies is from this point of view hazardous as well as useless. Similarly, the Homeric style and scale of the rewards promised is out of accord with the Virgilian context—two silver cups, two tripods, two talents of gold, a mixing bowl, and (after final victory) the horse and armour of Turnus, twelve female slaves with children, and the whole private lands of king Latinus himself: the recipients of these do not belong to the Homeric world, and the gifts are as inappropriate as they would seem in the pages of Livy if offered by a Roman general to a patriotic volunteer.

It remains to consider two imperfections that are involved in the general design of the poem. The first of these can be briefly stated.

It is that the emphasis frequently laid during the story, and required by its basic conception, on the long duration and grievous weight of the trials endured by Aeneas and his party on their voyage from Troy to Italy is simply not sustained by the narrative of these trials, and this inadequacy is thrown into relief by the contrasted intensity of the suffering of Dido. The second major imperfection of design is this. In the middle of the poem the hero reaches the promised land, and receives a succession of supernatural reassurances: in the war that follows he is the destined victor and confident of his destiny, quelling a resistance which is doomed from the first to failure. Our concern for the hero and our interest in the 'Roman' significance of the *Aeneid* are both satisfied by the end of the eighth book, and the concluding books are from this point of view an anti-climax, though they engage our interest on behalf of the misguided but sincere resisters. It seems unlikely that Virgil intended the interest to shift so markedly from his hero in these last three books; for they would be to the mind of his age the most 'epic' part of all his story, the tale of *arma* promised in the *Aeneid*'s opening line. It is possible therefore that these last books with their tale of war had a significance for the poet and his readers which the modern reader misses; for instance, evocations of the then recent civil wars of Rome. But this of course is speculation. The diminution of interest is not due to a failure of the poet in dealing with a tale of war as such, for he had been successful in diversifying his narrative, on the one hand by blending with the obvious Homeric elements un-Homeric modernities such as the siege operations of Book 9 and the cavalry tactics of Book 11, but also by the variety of distinctive characters that he introduces, Nisus and Euryalus, Pallas, Lausus, Mezentius, Camilla and the rest. It is true, however, that the more exigent requirements of plot in this part of the *Aeneid* leave no scope for magnificent episodes, such as the tale of the fall of Troy, the fate of Dido and the descent into the world of the dead; and this contributes to the feeling of many modern readers feeling that the story's interest fades in its latter part. Fortunately the last scenes of all, in which Turnus realizes his failure and faces his death, are as splendid and powerful as any in the poem.

APPENDIX 5

A further note on echoes of contemporary history in the poem

THE facts cited in Chapter 10 make it clear that the narrative of the *Aeneid* is at some points coloured by reminiscence of events in the career of Octavian (or Augustus, as he became in 27 B.C. while Virgil was at work on his poem). It is hardly possible to determine how far this process is carried, and with what degree of intention. But it may be worth while to consider some factors bearing on the question, both in the background and in the evidence of the poem itself.

Virgil had announced in the prologue to his third *Georgic* the intention to make a poem on a grand scale that should honour Octavian down the ages. The great prophetic passages in the first and sixth and eighth books of the *Aeneid* display the historical process begun by Aeneas as culminating in the achievements of Octavian in the poet's own day, and both in these passages and in others we are reminded that Aeneas is also Octavian's ancestor.[1] The restoration of peace and order after the civil wars would naturally ensure to the victor the admiration and affection of the majority who benefited by it. 'After twenty years', wrote one admirer, 'the civil wars were ended, and wars with foreign enemies laid to rest. Peace returned; armed strife and its passions were everywhere stilled; the rule of law was restored . . . the land began to be cultivated again, the worship of the gods to be duly observed, and the individual citizen felt once more secure and safe in the possession of his property' (Velleius Paterculus 2.89). The same feeling is expressed in the last of Horace's *Odes* (4.15) and in more than one passage of the *Aeneid* itself. It is thus not surprising that Octavian should be much in mind in all the *Aeneid*, which was composed in the ten years immediately following the end of the civil wars. This implies no sycophancy or insincerity in the poet, for he and the world had much to be grateful for. Moreover the personal magnetism of Octavian is attested by Suetonius and amply confirmed by Octavian's hold on his soldiers and lieutenants. It appears further from the terms of a letter which the emperor wrote to Virgil from Spain in the year 25 B.C. or thereabouts (see p. 118 above), and from the fact that Virgil joined him

at Athens on his return from the East in 19 B.C.—the occasion of the
illness that led to the poet's death—that the relations between the
two were more intimate than official. At the same time, neither
friendship nor gratitude would oblige the poet to be blind or indifferent to ugly aspects of Octavian's early career which were of
common knowledge and regretted later by Octavian himself. 'He
was', says a later writer, 'a merciful ruler, if one considers his career
from the beginning of his principate', but also 'as a young man he
was subject to fits of angry passion, and did many things which it
pained him later to recall' (Seneca, *Clementia* 1.9.1 and 11.1).

Against this background it is not surprising that echoes of the
person of Octavian and of events in his career should be felt in the
Aeneid. For just as Virgil's creative imagination works with material
drawn from previous literature, with Homer as most immediate and
pervasive source, so we might expect it to draw on ideas suggested
by history, and especially on the most impressive fact of history in
the poet's experience, namely the career of Octavian. That precisely
this does in some cases happen we have already seen. The question
is of the extent to which it happens.

A convenient method of considering this is by grouping the instances to be examined in two different ways; first with reference to
certain extraordinary occasions in Octavian's career, and then again
with reference to certain more general aspects of that career which
we know were emphasized by his admirers.

One extraordinary occasion was the return of Octavian to Rome
in 29 B.C. after he had brought the civil wars to a final conclusion
and removed the peril of foreign domination supposed to be represented by the association of Cleopatra with his rival Antony. His
triumph on that occasion and the national rejoicing are explicitly
introduced in the scene on the shield of Aeneas at the end of the
eighth book of the *Aeneid*. But we have seen that reminiscences of the
honours paid him then have also coloured the account in the same
book of the celebrations in honour of Hercules held by Evander and
his Arcadians: the libations, the Salian hymn, the thanksgiving of
the people for liberation from a monstrous peril. After the triumph
came the dedication of the temple to Octavian's adoptive father
Julius, now deified as Divus Julius, and the games in his honour,
which included an exhibition of the *Lusus Troiae*. A reminiscence of
these (and also of the games held in the same Julius' honour in
44 B.C., when the comet appeared) has, as we have also seen,
coloured and perhaps inspired the account of Aeneas' games for

Anchises in the fifth book of the *Aeneid*, with the associated reference
to Anchises as *divinus* and promise of the dedication of a temple to
him. It is clear that the events of 29 B.C. have left their impression
on the *Aeneid* indirectly as well as directly.

Two years later, in 27 B.C., came another extraordinary occasion:
the dramatic offer of Octavian to restore the Republic, for which he
was honoured with the dedication of the golden shield in the senate-
house and the oak-crown fixed for ever above his door. We have seen
that the act of Octavian is apparently recalled in the terms of
Aeneas' disclaimer of personal ambition at the truce-making in the
last book of the *Aeneid*; and that the shield and the oak-crown are
very probably recalled in the eighth book in the shield which Venus
brings with the rest of the god-made armour and the oak by which
she sets them down. There was another striking event which marked
the same occasion in 27 B.C., a phenomenal rise of the Tiber which
flooded the lower-lying parts of Rome in the night, at the time of
Octavian's offer and the decreeing of honours to him on account of
it (Dio Cassius, 53.20). It may be that there is a reminiscence of this
in the passage, also in the eighth book, in which the Tiber is said
(8.86–7) to have stilled his stream 'which all that night had been in
spate', in order to afford Aeneas and his men an easy passage to
Evander's settlement on the site of future Rome. For else why the
particulars about the exceptional spate, when for the river to have
checked its flow would have been sufficient for the context? (However, this passage is construed by many editors of Virgil in a different
way.)

The events of 29 and 27 B.C. discussed above happened while
Virgil was actually working on the *Aeneid*, and it is natural that they
should leave their impression. Another set of events that may also
have left their impression, for a different reason, occurred in con-
nexion with the war against Sextus Pompeius in 38–6 B.C., about ten
years earlier. This war was attended by exceptional hazards for
Octavian, whose forces twice suffered defeat in sea-battles and were
twice shattered by storm. Similarities have been noted between
Appian's account (*Civil War* 5.88–90 and 98–9) of some of these
events and passages in the first and fifth books of the *Aeneid*, especially the description of the storm and its sequel in the first book.[2]
Some of these are too general to be conclusive, but they are interesting in the light of the fact that Appian is known to have used the
emperor's memoirs, and that the main base of operations for the
Caesarian navy was in and about Puteoli, and so in the near neigh-

bourhood of Naples where Virgil commonly resided at this time. The following comparisons may serve for specimens. In Appian 5.98 we read 'Caesar sailed from Puteoli, making sacrifice and libation from the flagship into the sea . . .'; and at *Aeneid* 5.772 ff. 'Aeneas himself stood apart on the prow, holding a cup, and cast the entrails of the victims into the brine and poured libations of sparkling wine'. Again, in Appian 5.117 Octavian and his army, having landed in Sicily, are overtaken by night on their march, 'and there were angry sounds of thunder from Etna and long rumblings and flashes of fire about the army, so that some (of the troops) leaped up in terror, while those who knew about Etna thought that at any minute . . .'; similarly in *Aeneid* 3.583 ff. it is said of the Trojans near Etna that 'we took shelter in the woods and all that night long suffered fearful terrors, and could not tell what made the noise'. Again, Suetonius (*Aug.* 16) mentions that just before the final sea-fight Octavian was 'suddenly overpowered' by sleep, like Palinurus in the extraordinary episode at the end of the fifth book of the *Aeneid*. In all of these instances the scene or event is remarkable, and the presence of it in the *Aeneid* not due to anything in the legend or in known literary precedent, whereas an obviously possible source is reminiscence of events of the war of 38–36 B.C. But if we suppose that such reminiscence has in fact supplied material here to Virgil's imagination, it does not seem likely that this was intended by the poet to have an evocative effect, as may well have been the case with the events of 29 and 27 B.C. Similarly Virgil's reminiscences of Homer are sometimes clearly intended to evoke a memory of a Homeric passage, but sometimes have done no more than provide part of the raw material out of which the poet's imagination constructs his story.

Turning to more general aspects of the question, one may note that the figure of Hercules in Book 8 is evocative of qualities of Octavian additional to those noted above. Hercules and Octavian are both 'saviours' (8.189 *servati*; Propertius 4.6.37 *mundi servator*), and qualified for divinity (8.301 *decus addite divis*; *Georg.* 1.24 *tu . . . quem mox quae sint habitura deorum concilia incertum est*), as also is Aeneas (12.794 *Aenean scis . . . deberi caelo* etc.). And when Aeneas comes to enter Evander's modest dwelling on the Palatine, he is exhorted by his host to be content like Hercules before him with its simplicity and so 'to make yourself deserving of godhead' (8.364 *te quoque dignum finge deo*). There can be no doubt that these words in this setting not only suggest the prospective deification of Aeneas, and of Octavian, but also recall the simplicity of Octavian-Augustus' living arrangements, remarked on by Suetonius (*Aug.* 72–3); 'he lived on the Palatine, but still in the modest house which had belonged to Hortensius, remarkable neither for size or ornamentation . . . the plainness of the furniture can still be observed . . . simpler if anything than that of a private citizen'. Again, when Aeneas is saluted (8.513) by Evander as (*Teucrum atque*) *Italum fortissime ductor*, the wording seems to echo Octavian's claim, recorded in the Res Gestae (25), that *tota Italia . . . me . . . ducem depoposcit*. Again, the inspiration afforded to Aeneas by the spirit of his dead father (6.806 *et dubitamus adhuc virtutem extendere factis, aut metus Ausonia prohibet consistere terra?*) corresponds to the inspiration drawn by Octavian from his adoptive father Julius (Vell. Pat. 2.60.2 '. . . declaring that it would be intolerable that he should not think himself worthy of the name that Caesar had thought him worthy of'). Again, the words with which Anchises greets Aeneas at their meeting in the underworld—*et tua demum vicit iter durum pietas?*—repeat (though in a very different context) the admiration of Caesar for the courage and energy his nephew showed in following him to Spain in 45 B.C. (Suet. *Aug.* 8 *avunculum . . . per infestas hostibus vias subsecutus magno opere demeruit, approbata cito etiam morum indole super itineris industriam*). Examples could be multiplied.

Considering the evident reminiscences of Octavian's regard for his adoptive father in the filial piety of Aeneas towards Anchises, not only in some of the above examples but also and more specifically in the episode of the funeral games in Book 5, one might expect an allusion in the *Aeneid* to the motive which Octavian claimed was dominant with him in all the early years of his career, namely, to avenge Julius Caesar's death. 'He thought it his first duty to avenge the death of his (great-)uncle (and adoptive father)' says Suetonius (*Aug.* 10), and so too Ovid: 'this was Caesar's first duty, his first undertaking in manhood, to avenge his father's death with righteous arms' (*Fasti*, 3.709). The expectation of an allusion to this is increased by the fact that the war in Italy in the last half of the *Aeneid* reflects in some respects the civil wars of Rome. And in fact the allusion *is* present, in the vengeance Aeneas seeks and takes on Turnus for the death of his friend Pallas. This corresponds evidently enough to the vengeance taken by Achilles in the *Iliad* on Hector for the death of Patroclus. And it is made an allusion to the vengeance of Octavian on the murderers of Caesar by the fact that Octavian was known to have quoted the words of Achilles in the *Iliad* (18.98–9) to those who counselled caution to him after Caesar's death: 'may I die here and now, since I failed my friend and was not there to save him when he fell', and he went on to declare that Caesar was not only friend to him but comrade in arms and commander as well (Appian, *Civil War*, 3.3). Thus Caesar the father is represented in the *Aeneid* by Anchises, and Caesar the fallen friend and comrade in arms is represented by Pallas. And in this must lie the explanation of the savagery of Aeneas after the death of Pallas (pp. 28–9 above), in accord with the primitive fury of an Achilles to be sure, but strangely discordant with the normally disciplined humanity of Aeneas. For Seneca says, it will be remembered, that Octavian was 'a mild and humane ruler, if one judges by his conduct in his principate; but as a young man he yielded to passion at times and did many things which he did not care to think of afterwards'. It was believed (Suet. *Aug.* 15), rightly or not, that after the fall of Perusia in 41 B.C. he caused three hundred knights and senators to be slaughtered like sacrificial victims at an altar erected in honour of the dead Julius. It is difficult to understand the act of Aeneas in taking and sending prisoners to be sacrificed at Pallas' funeral, except in the light of this story. The precedent of Achilles' similar act in the *Iliad* (21.27 ff. and 23. 175–6) will not alone account for it; for human sacrifice is called by Livy 'un-Roman', and Aeneas is conceived in general by Virgil as humane by nature as well as controlled by self-discipline.

It will be seen from this that the allusions to contemporary events and persons in the *Aeneid* do not follow a consistent pattern of equivalences. Octavian is suggested sometimes by Aeneas, sometimes by Hercules. Julius Caesar is recalled in some aspects by Anchises, father of the hero, sometimes by Pallas his slain friend. This is not far different from the way in which the reflections of Homeric characters in the *Aeneid* shift and combine. Turnus reflects now Achilles, now Hector. Aeneas reflects now the Homeric Aeneas, now the Homeric Achilles. Virgil's mind in relation to history and to literary precedent alike is less like a mirror than a kaleidoscope. Yet this may be an over-simplification and it may be that the person of Aeneas, though not a mirror image of Octavian, is a nearer reflection than has been implied above. Dio Cassius in his account of the history of this period, written it is true two centuries later, puts in the mouth of Octavian on the occasion of his professed offer to restore the republic in 27 B.C. a speech which though fictitious may well go back in its outline to a contemporary version, perhaps from Livy. A part of it (D.C. 53.4) runs as follows: '. . . that the facts themselves may satisfy you that I had no desire for supreme power on my own account, but that in very truth my object was to avenge the wicked murder of my father and to save the state from the great evils which then continually beset it. For I would far rather that the commonwealth had never had need of me for this, but that we like our forebears could have dwelt in peace and concord with one another . . . But since Destiny, as it seems, brought it about that you should have need of me, young still though I then was, . . . I let nothing deter me from coming to your aid in your time of peril, not weariness, nor fear, nor the threats of enemies, nor the entreaties of friends, nor the number of those leagued against us, nor the desperate fury of our adversaries, but I set myself unsparingly to brave every hazard, and I did and suffered those things of which you know.' In the same historian's version of the funeral speech pronounced over the emperor by his successor Tiberius it is said (D.C. 56.53) that in the civil wars 'he did and suffered not what he himself desired but what was willed by the power that rules the world'. The picture here of a man who was agent of destiny, who had no personal ambitions, who endured for the good of his country great labours and great perils, undeterred by the appeals of friends and undismayed by the number and desperate fury of his adversaries, might be an account of the hero of the *Aeneid*, even in the implied acknowledgement of some acts that he regretted. It may be therefore that in outline the character of Aeneas in the *Aeneid* is in fact drawn from Virgil's conception of that of Octavian-Augustus. But about this we can only speculate, for we do not know what lies behind the speech in Dio.

REFERENCES AND NOTES

CHAPTER I

1. 1.257 ff.; 6.756 ff.; 8.626 ff.

2. See Chapter X and Appendix 5.

3. See *Life* (in Appendix 1), and Horace, *Epistles* 2.1.246.

4. See *Life* (in Appendix 1).

5. See (for instance) J. H. Hanford, *A Milton Handbook*, pp. 181 ff., or the *Life of Milton* in Johnson's *Lives of the Poets*.

6. See *Life* (Appendix 1), and Aulus Gellius 17.10.1–7.

7. See Chapter VI.

8. Ovid, *Tristia* 4.10.25–6; Cicero, *Archias* 18; cf. Cicero, *De Oratore* 3.194, where the same kind of facility is attributed to Antipater of Sidon (2nd century B.C.).

9. See Appendix 3.

10. See Chapter XI.

11. See Appendix 3.

12. A good statement of this view is in W. Warde Fowler, *Religious Experience of the Roman People* (1911), ch. 18.

13. 6.889.

14. See also Chapter VI.

15. 8.200–1.

16. 5.3–4.

17. See J. Gagé, *Actiaca*, pp. 85–6, in *Mélanges d'Archéologie et d'Histoire*, 1936. I owe the reference to Professor Alföldi and Dr. Higgins.

18. Regarding Neptune, see last note; regarding Hercules, see Book 8 of the *Aeneid* and Chapter X below.

CHAPTER II

1. Auctor ad Herennium 4.46.

2. Neptune, 5.817 ff. (also 1.142 ff.). Vulcan, 8.406 ff. Rumour, 4.173 ff. Allecto, 7.324 ff. Cacus, 8.193 ff. The Dira, 12.845 ff.

3. The storm in 1 (cf. *Odyssey* 5); the games in 5 (cf. *Iliad* 23); the underworld in 6 (cf. *Odyssey* 11); the catalogue of troops in 7 (cf. *Iliad* 2); the marvellous shield in 8 (cf. *Iliad* 18); the night adventure in 9 (cf. *Iliad* 10); the duel to the death between the rival heroes in 12 (cf. *Iliad* 22).

4. 3.293 ff. and 11.225 ff.

5. The cloaked head, 3.403 ff., 545. The *lusus Troiae*, 5.596 ff. The Sibylline Books, 6.71 ff. The Gates of Janus, 7.601 ff. The Great Altar of Hercules, 8.268–72. The funeral procession, 11.59 ff. and 139 ff. (this last is not explicitly said to correspond to later Roman custom, but in numerous particulars can be shown to do so).

6. 3.521 ff.

7. For the correspondences between this building and the Capitoline temple see further in note 14 on p. 153.

8. Cacus, 8.185 ff. Picus, 7.189 ff. Cycnus, 10.189 ff. Caeculus, 7.678 ff.

9. See Cicero, *Sestius* 67; Brutus in Cicero, *Epp. ad Brutum* 24.2; Ovid, *Fasti* 1.85–6; etc. It will be seen from this that phrases such as 1.278–9 *his ego nec metas rerum nec tempora pono; imperium sine fine dedi*, or 4.229 ff. *sed fore qui . . . totum sub leges mitteret orbem*, or 6.794–5 *super et Garamantas et Indos proeferet imperium* are not to be understood as claiming a divine sanction for aspirations to world conquest. And in fact Roman policy in Virgil's day was concerned with security rather than expansion; and Augustus' advice to his successor was (Tacitus, *Annals* 1.11 etc.) *not* to advance the empire's existing frontiers.

10. 'Our manifest destiny to overspread the continent allotted by Providence for the free development of our yearly multiplying millions', J. O'Sullivan, in the *U.S. Magazine and Democratic Review*, 1845.
'Take up the white man's burden . . .' etc., Rudyard Kipling, in a poem written in 1899.

'We are the salt of the earth. God has called us to civilise the world', the
Emperor William II, in a speech at Bremen in 1902 (according to J. Burnet,
Essays and Addresses, 1929, p. 176).

11. Anchises' words at 6.851 ff. *tu regere imperio populos, Romane, memento . . .*
etc. are simply a prophecy of the Roman empire as Virgil knew it; and there
is no reason to assign any different meaning to the words of Jupiter at
4.229 ff. I do not think there is any evidence that the Romans conceived
themselves as having a 'mission' to improve the world, though very probably
they did improve it. Aeneas in the *Aeneid* has indeed a 'mission' to found the
race from which Rome is to spring; but that is quite a different matter.

12. Propertius 4.1.59; Livy, *Praefatio* 3.

13. Cicero, *Brutus* 253–4; also *De Natura Deorum* 1.7–8; *De Divinatione* 2.1;
Tusc. Disp. 1.5–6; *De Finibus* 1.10; cf. *De Legibus* 1.5.

14. Propertius 2.34.66.

15. See 6.96–7; 11.24–8; 3.500 ff.

CHAPTER III

1. Statues of national worthies, Suetonius, *Aug.* 31 and *Calig.* 34. Busts of
distinguished ancestors, Pliny, *Nat. Hist.* 35.6. Enumerations of famous
names, Cicero, *Caelius* 39; *Sestius* 143; *Tusc. Disp.* 1.110.

2. 12.166.

3. Fate's purpose (above), 1.2; 1.205; 1.382. Fate's command (here),
6.461 ff.; 7.240; 3.494.

4. 1.33 and 12.177.

5. Trial and affliction, 1.3; 6.693; 3.182; 5.725.

6. An 'abiding city' etc., 3.86; 3.97 etc.

7. Progressive revelation, 3.7; 3.94 ff.; 3.147 ff.; 3.374 ff.; 5.735–7 and
6.716 ff.

8. *Genesis* 12.1–4; *Hebrews* 11.8–10.

9. Plato, *Apology* 30A and 33C.

10. See 8.288 ff. and Chapter X below.

11. Aeneas (4.265 ff.) is reminded and commanded; Dido (1.715 ff., 4.90) and Turnus (7.445 ff.) are *possessed*.

12. 5.700–3.

13. Anxiety, 1.208; 8.19; 5.701; 10.217; 8.522.

14. Fatigue, 3.496; 5.629; 1.437; 3.493 ff.

15. 1.92 and 12.945–51.

16. 2.314–7.

17. 4.332 and 395 and 448 (note *per*sentit).

18. 10.510 ff., 569 ff., 603–4.

19. 5.770; 6.332; 10.821–3; 11.2–3; 5.350 and 463–4.

20. 1.220; 1.305; 4.393.

21. 5.286, 418; 6.176, 232; 7.5; 11.170.

22. 1.378.

23. See for example 2.718–19; 3.19, 62, 84, 176–8, 279, 543–7; 5.743; 7.133–47; 8.68–85, 541–4; 10.251–5; 11.1 ff.; 12.175 ff.

24. 3.709; 5.731 ff.; 6.106 ff., 403 ff., 687–8.

25. The role of Anchises in relation to Aeneas' mission: 3.9, 472; 4.351; 5.722 ff.; 6.716 ff., 888–9; 7.133–4.

26. 2.432–4.

27. 2.314.

28. Apparition of Hector, 2.270 ff.; of Venus, 2.589 ff.; of Creusa, 2.771 ff.

29. 1.198 ff., 453 ff., 381 ff.

30. 6.83.

31. 7.117–47.

32. 8.31 ff.

33. The new *patria*: 1.205 and 380; 4.347; 11.25.

34. The awaited man of destiny: 7.270–3; 8.512; 8.38.

35. Assurances: 8.40–1; 8.523 ff. and 612 ff.; 8.513; cf. also 10.241–5.

36. Aeneas' confidence: 8.537 ff.; 10.250 ff.; 10.875–6; 12.108–12; cf. also 11.14; 12.565.

37. 'An unholy war': 7.583–4; and cf. 11.232–3; 12.31. Juno's perversity; 7.313 ff.

38. 11.112; 12.190–4.

39. 10.557; 10.517 ff. and 11.81–2; cf. also more generally the whole tone of the passage 10.510–604.

40. The Homeric precedent is the sacrifice of prisoners by Achilles on Patroclus' pyre (*Iliad* 23.175 f.). For contemporary Roman views see Cicero, *Fonteius* 31 *illam immanem et barbaram consuetudinem hominum immolandorum*; Livy 22.57.6 . . . *hostiis humanis, minime Romano sacro* (where Livy is disapproving as exceptional a sacrifice actually done at Rome in a time of panic long before).

41. Compare 4.395 with 4.281 (however, *magno . . . amore* in 395, by most understood of Aeneas' feelings, is sometimes taken to refer to his realization of the intensity of Dido's).

42. Cicero, *Tusc. Disp.* 4.69 . . . *amorem, flagitii et levitatis auctorem.*

43. See Plutarch, *Antony*, and (for example) Horace, *Odes* 1.37.5 ff., Propertius 3.11.29 ff.

44. 4.221; 4.193–4.

45. Florus 2.21.3 *patriae, nominis, togae, fascium oblitus totus in monstrum illud ut mente ita amictu quoque cultuque desciverat: aureum in manu baculum, in latere acinaces, purpurea vestis ingentibus obstricta gemmis.*

46. Catullus 85.

CHAPTER IV

1. Aeneas in the role of Dido's consort, 4.260 ff.

2. The call, if it is not illusory anyway, will appear to her to come from the gods of Troy; and she is a Carthaginian.

3. 'Aeneas becomes uneasy': that this was so before the warning is inferred from 4.351 ff., where he says that his sleep has been troubled by dreams of his father and the thought of his son. It may be however that some days have elapsed between the warning and the scene with Dido in which 351 ff. stand; in which case the dreams etc. may have come after the warning and not before.

4. Dido's thoughts of death: 4.308, 323, 385, 436, 451, 460, 475, 519, 547, 630 ff.

5. 4.547.

6. 11.72 ff.

7. Juno, 1.12 ff., 50 ff.; Jupiter, 1.297 ff.; Venus, 1.657–722; Juno, 4.90–170; Jupiter, 4.220–77.

8. With this and the above cf. 4.321 ff., 27 ff., 552, 221, 65–89, 534.

9. Dido's self-spoken epitaph, 4.651–8. With the manner may be compared that of the Epitaphs of the Scipios, most easily to be found in the *Oxford Book of Latin Verse*, p. 3.

10. Already at 1.712 she is *pesti devota futurae*, and receives for the first time the epithet *infelix*, which recurs thereafter throughout the story: 1.749; 4.68, 450, 529, 596; 5.3; 6.456.

11. Aeneas' prayer, 1.603 ff.

12. The original legend of Dido as given by Pompeius Trogus (a contemporary of Virgil) is epitomized in Justinus 18.4–6. A closely similar version was given by Timaeus (third century B.C.), fr.23 (Mueller). Macrobius 5.17.5–6 refers to Virgil's story as *fabula lascivientis Didonis, quam falsam novit universitas*, and continues: *tantum valuit pulcritudo narrandi ut omnes, Phoenissae castitatis conscii nec ignari manum sibi iniecisse reginam ne pateretur damnum pudoris, coniveant tamen fabulae et . . . malint pro vero celebrari quod pectoribus humanis dulcedo fingentis infudit.*

13. 7.365–6.

14. 9.757 ff.

15. 11.901–5.

16. Turnus' shame: 12.638–45, 666–7, 679–80.

17. Juno's perversity: 7.313–19; 12.149–51.

18. 7.413–61.

19. *amens*: 7.460; 12.622 etc. *turbidus*: 9.57; 10.648; 12.10, 671. *fervidus*: 9.72; 12.325. *ardens*: 9.760; 12.3, 71, 101, 325, 732. *furor, furens* etc.: 9.691, 760; 11.486, 901; 12.680. *violentia, violentus*: 10.151; 11.354, 376; 12.9, 45.

20. 9.730 ff., 760 ff.; 12.324 ff.; 9.760; 11.901.

21. Turnus' realization, 12.614–95.

22. 9.1–24.

23. 7.583–4.

24. Manlius Torquatus, Livy 7.10.11–3.

25. Pallas himself had hoped to strip Turnus of his arms, 10.462.

26. With the above cf. 12.29; 7.473–4; 11.222–4; 10.672; 12.638 ff.; 12.694–5; 7.365–6; 7.423–6; 10.79.

27. With the above cf. 7.531 ff.; 10.75; 7.469.

28. 12.646–9.

29. 10.617 and 630–1.

30. *Aen.* 1.294–6; Horace, *Odes* 4.15.17–8; Cicero, (e.g.) *Philippics* 2.68 *ut es violentus et furens*; 5.19 *homo vehemens et violentus*; 5.23 *ille furens*; 5.37 *homo amentissimus . . . eius furorem . . .*; 5.43 *furori M. Antoni*; 12.26 *novi hominis furorem, novi effrenatam violentiam*; 13.18 *inde se quo furore, quo ardore . . . ad urbem rapiebat.*

CHAPTER V

1. Palinurus, 5.833 ff. Arruns, 11.849 ff.

2. The numinous presence on the Capitol, 8.347–54.

3. Ovid, *Ars* 1.637 *expedit esse deos et, ut expedit, esse putemus.*

4. 8.398–9.

5. 12.819 ff.

6. In one place, 10.112–3 *rex Iuppiter omnibus idem: fata viam invenient,* Jupiter appears, by his own choice, as an observer, while fate's ordinances find their fulfilment without his assistance. This does not imply that he does not know what these are (cf. 1.257–62) or that his will is not in agreement with them. It does imply that he is not their author, in the poet's conception at this moment.

7. 12.429.

8. 5.235–43.

9. 1.131 ff.; 12.766–87.

10. Minucius Felix, *Octavius* 6 *sic eorum potestas et auctoritas totius orbis ambitus occupavit, sic imperium suum ultra solis vias et ipsius oceani limites propagavit, dum exercent in armis virtutem religiosam, dum urbem muniunt sacrorum religionibus, castis virginibus, multis honoribus ac nominibus sacerdotum.* . . . (c. A.D. 200)
Q. Aurelius Symmachus (ed. Seeck, p. 280) *Roman nunc putemus adsistere atque his vobiscum agere sermonibus:* '*Optimi principum, patres patriae, reveremini annos meos, in quos me pius ritus adduxit. utar caerimoniis avitis; neque enim paenitet.* . . . *hic cultus in leges meas orbem redegit, haec sacra Hannibalem a moenibus, a Capitolio Senones reppulerunt.* . . . (A.D. 384)

11. For references see note 23 on p. 147.

12. 3.435 ff. and 546–7; 8.59 ff. and 81 ff.; 12.818–41.

13. Cicero, *De Natura Deorum* 3.5 . . . *nostrae civitatis, quae nunquam profecto sine summa placatione deorum immortalium tanta esse potuisset.*

14. *Georg.* 2.491; *Aen.* 8.334.

15. 6.332 and 376.

16. 6.882.

17. Neptune, 1.124 ff. Vulcan, 8.388 ff. Cybele, 9.82 ff. Diana, 11.532 ff. Juno, 1.15 ff. etc.

18. The passages referred to here and above are: Laocoon, 2.199 ff., 228 ff.; Iris and the Trojan women, 5.643 ff.; Iris and Turnus, 9.1 ff.; the portent which deceives the Latins, 12.244 ff., 259–60.

19. The passages referred to here and above are: the Trojans' thanksgivings, 2.248–9; Aeneas' prayer, 1.603–4; Dido's prayer at the banquet, 1.731–3; Dido's prayer for help in her extremity, 4.520–1.

20. The passages referred to here and above are: Troy, 3.2; Turnus, 10.630; Dido, 6.475; Palinurus, 5.841.

21. Thus Cicero (*De Officiis* 3.102) says that 'all philosophers agree that God is never angry and never harms'. But also (*De Divinatione* 2.148) that that 'widespread superstition has almost all mankind in thrall'. He defines superstition elsewhere (*De Natura Deorum* 1.117) as importing an irrational fear of the supernatural.

22. Tibullus 1.10.15–16; Juvenal 12.89–90.

23. Lucretius 5.1194 *o genus infelix humanum, talia divis cum tribuit facta atque iras adiunxit acerbas;* 5.1233 *usque adeo res humanas vis abdita quaedam obterit, et pulcros fasces saevasque secures proculcare et ludibrio sibi habere videtur.*

24. Horace, *Odes* 3.29.49–50.

25. Epicurus, *Letter to Menoeceus*, in Diogenes Laertius 10.134.

26. Pliny, *Nat. Hist.* 2.14–24.

27. Apuleius, *Metamorphoses* 11.25.

28. *Pantheon* (Ed. H. Kleinknecht, Stuttgart, 1929), pp. 68–9.

29. For this view of Hercules see Cicero, *De Officiis* 3.25 . . . *pro omnibus genti-bus conservandis aut iuvandis maximos labores suscipere, imitantem Herculem illum, quem hominum fama beneficiorum memor in concilio caelestium collocavit;* cf. *De Finibus* 2.119; 3.66; Horace, *Odes* 3.3.9.

30. 8.200–1.

CHAPTER VI

1. For further illustration see the articles in the *Oxford Classical Dictionary* on Aratus (of Soli), Theocritus, Callimachus, Euphorion, and the general article on Alexandrian Poetry.

2. *Poetics*, ch. 7.

3. *Poetics*, ch. 23.

4. Compare 1.34–49 and 50 ff. with 7.286–322 and 323 ff.; also 4.705 with 12.952.

5. 6.83 and 86 ff.

6. *Eclogues* 6.3; Horace, *Odes* 4.15.1–2.

7. 7.41 ff.

8. Vulcan, 8.370 ff.

9. Neptune, 5.779 ff.

10. Apparition of the Tiber-god, 8.26 ff.

11. Apparition of Anchises, 5.721 ff.

12. Journey's End reached 7.107–47.

13. Prophecies of the Trojans' coming, 7.68 ff. and 98 ff.; speeches of Trojan envoys and Latinus, 7.192–285.

14. The correspondences between this building (*Aeneid* 7.170–86) and the Capitoline temple are both numerous and precise. The Capitoline temple was vast and majestic (*augustum, ingens*). It stood conspicuous on a hill. It was fronted with a *triple* row of columns (Dionysius of Halicarnassus, *Roman Antiquities*, 4.61). It was no doubt adorned, as was common practice, with spoils of war (Livy, 40.51; *Aeneid*, 8.721). At its entrance stood statues of former kings (Appian, *Civil War*, 1.16) and heroes (Suetonius, *Cal.* 34). It was the scene of meetings of the senate (e.g. at the beginning of the year, Livy, 24.10; for the recall of Cicero, *De Domo* 14). It was the scene on 13 September and 13 November each year of the ritual banquet called the *epulum Iovis*, in which the senate took part (Valerius Maximus, 2.1.2; Aulus Gellius, 12.8 *cum sollemni die epulum Iovis libaretur atque ob id sacrificium senatus in Capitolio epularetur*). It was the scene of the assumption of office by the

consuls of the Republic and their first appearance with lictors carrying the *fasces* before them as symbol of their authority (Ovid, *Fasti* 1.79 ff).

15. Signs and assurances: the bough, 6.146–7; the tables, 7.116 ff.; the thunder-clap, 7.141 ff.; the sow, 8.39 ff. and 81 ff.; the glitter of arms in the sky and the trumpet-blast, 8.524 ff.

16. Miraculously assisted progress to Italy 5.800–26; to the Tiber-estuary 7.8–36; to the site of Rome 8.86–96.

17. Interventions of Iris, 5.606 ff. and 9.2 ff.

18. The passages referred to above are: Mnestheus, 5.188 ff. and 9.781 ff.; Nisus and Euryalus, 5.294 ff. and 9.176 ff.; Ascanius, 5.545 ff., 664 ff., and 9.256 ff., 622 ff.

19. See Appendix 1.

20. Catullus, 64.52 ff. and 251 ff. (the opening and closing scenes).

21. Catullus, 64.76 ff. and 212 ff. (the two narratives), and 124–206 (the lament of Ariadne).

22. See notes 5 and 3 on p. 145; also pp. 54–6. For the name of Rome, see 5.123, 601; 6.781, 789, 810, 851, 857; 7.603; 8.99, 313, 361, 624, 635; 9.449;

CHAPTER VII

1. Examples of Ennian phrasing: 3.163; 9.532; 12.18; 4.576; 7.622; 7.625; 9.165; 7.520; 11.745; 10.2; 6.846.
   Paraphrases of homely processes: e.g. 1.174 ff.; 6.6–7; 7.109–15.

2. 9.455; 9.163; 5.139.

3. 6.353; 10.269; 1.260.

4. 5.380; 2.83; 5.505; 11.82.

5. 7.684; 11.180; 11.512.

6. 5.119; 3.428; 6.887; 4.178; 6.446.

7. 1.519; 12.928; 7.433; 2.336; 6.225; 3.618.

8. 11.750; 8.365; 6.457; 12.665; 1.460; 12.43.

9. 3.145–6; 5.655–6.

10. 2.551; 6.360; 10.383; 4.586; 2.301; 8.446.

11. 1.725.

12. 2.528.

13. 10.227.

14. *ingens*: 1.640; 8.252; 12.268; 7.241; 10.541.

15. *cavus*: 2.487; 5.434; 12.85–6; 9.633; 6.293; 2.360.

16. This has recently been studied in detail, with instructive results, by
G. E. Duckworth in *T.P.A.P.A.* 95 (1964).

17. The lines quoted are 4.486 and 1.105. The statement about absence of
coincidence of ictus and accent in *dat latus: insequitur cumulo praeruptus aquae
mons* is perhaps over-confident, as it is possible that some word groups (such
as (?) *dat latus*, (?) *aquae mons*) could be accented as if the group were a single
word. This would produce coincidence in the first and fifth and sixth feet in
this line.

18. I *Corinthians* 13; *Oxford Book of English Prose* 409 (p. 694).

19. Twilight, 6.272.

20. Shooting stars, 5.527. Lightning, 8.392.

21. 9.669; 12.451; 9.710; 7.587; 11.624.

22. 6.226; 6.227; 11.212; 2.609; 5.666.

23. 6.413 and 493.

24. 8.90 ff. and 455–6.

25. 4.86–9.

26. 12.928; 2.551.

27. 4.586 ff.; 12.669 ff.

28. F. W. H. Myers, in *Essays (Classical)*, 1883.

CHAPTER VIII

1. Regarding the Servian commentary see Appendix 1.

2. Regarding the progressive enlightenment of the Trojans about their destination, see p. 22 and note 7 on p. 146.

3. It appears from the few surviving fragments of Naevius' *Bellum Punicum*, his poem on the historical war between Rome and Carthage, that he told somewhere in it of Aeneas' departure from Troy and coming to Italy, and mentioned somewhere in it the foundress of Carthage, Dido. According to the Servian commentary on *Aen.* 4.682 and 5.4 Virgil's older contemporary Varro somewhere said that 'Anna' killed herself for love of Aeneas or —merely—was in love with him. And at an unknown date in the first century B.C. Ateius Philologus wrote an essay on the subject *An Didun amaverit Aeneas.*

4. Ap. Rhod. *Argonautica* 2.802 ff., 814.

5. The Fall of Troy came in the lost *Iliou Persis*, the story of the Amazon Penthesilea in the lost *Aethiopis.*

6. G. N. Knauer, *Die Aeneis und Homer* (1964), will be invaluable to anyone more closely concerned with this question in future. M. Hügi, *Vergils Aeneis und die Hellenistische Dichtung* (1952), is very helpful on the relationship between the *Aeneid* and Apollonius Rhodius' *Argonautica.*

CHAPTER IX

1. For references see note 1 on p. 146 above.

2. 6.724–34; cf. Cicero, *Rep.* 6.15 *his . . . animus datus est ex illis sempiternis ignibus, quae sidera et stellas vocatis, quae globosae et rotundae, divinis animatae mentibus . . . etc.*; 14 *immo vero, inquit, ei vivunt qui e corporum vinculis tamquam e carcere evolaverunt.*

3. 6.889 and cf. 718; Cicero, *Rep.* 6.13 *quo sis, Africane, alacrior ad tutandam rempublicam.*

4. The clearest evidence is Tertullian's (*De Anima* 56): 'they say that the prematurely dead must wander around until they reach the age at which they would have died in the course of nature'.

5. But the 'slain in war' evidently were one recognized category of the 'prematurely dead', for they appear in Lucian's *Cataplus* (6) in association

with 'executed persons' and 'suicides for love'. In Lucian's story these groups are about to cross the river in Charon's boat; unfortunately we do not learn what will happen to them afterwards.

6. The King of the Grove, Servius on *Aen.* 6.136, and J. G. Frazer, *The Golden Bough*, ch. 1. The Golden Fleece, Apollonius Rhodius, *Argonautica*, 4.123–6 and 162. The mistletoe, Pliny, *Nat. Hist.* 16.249 *signum electae ab ipso deo arboris*. The wand of the Initiate, scholiast on Aristophanes, *Knights*, 408 'the boughs which the Initiates carry in the Mysteries'. The dedication of a victor's palm to a god is attested by many inscriptions, and in Tibullus 1.9.82 such a palm is of gold, or gilt. Meleager's description of Plato's poem's as χρύσειον ἀεὶ θείοιο Πλάτωνος κλῶνα is in *Palatine Anthology*, 4.1.47–8.

CHAPTER X

1. Dido's curse, 4.622–9.

2. Compare 8.709 with 4.644.

3. 1.263–4 and 4.229–30.

4. 7.744–9; 9.603–13.

5. 7.583; 12.31; cf. Horace, *Odes* 2.1.30 *impia proelia* (the Civil Wars), and note 30 on p. 150.

6. 7.317.

7. Catullus 29.24 and *Aen.* 6.830–1.

8. 11.292 and 12.709.

9. 2.556–7.

10. Plutarch, *Pompey* 80.

11. Appian, *Civil War* 2.71.

12. Dionysius of Halicarnassus, *Roman Antiquities* 1.41–2; and compare Appian, *Illyrica* 15 and 16, where Octavian claims to have tamed 'certain barbarous tribes who have been harrying Italy'.

13. Propertius 4.6.37.

14. 8.189.

15. 8.200–1; *Ec.* 1.6 and 42–3; *Georg.* 1.24 ff.

16. Horace, *Odes* 3.3.9 ff.

17. Dio Cassius 51.19–21; *Res Gestae* 10.

18. Suetonius, *Aug.* 10, *Julius* 88; Pliny, *Nat. Hist.* 2.93; Appian, *Civil War* 3.28; Dio Cassius 45.6–7.

19. Dio Cassius 51.22.

20. 5.47 and 59.60.

21. 5.522–8.

22. Dio Cassius 51.22.

23. Suetonius, *Aug.* 43.

24. Pliny, *Nat. Hist.* 2.94, where Pliny quotes from Augustus' own memoirs: *iis ipsis ludorum meorum diebus sidus crinitum per septem dies in regione caeli quae sub septentrione est conspectum est. . . . eo sidere significari vulgus credidit Caesaris animam inter deorum immortalium numina receptam.* And Pliny himself adds: *interiore gaudio sibi illum* (sc. *cometen*) *natum seque in eo nasci interpretatus est.* It was an occasion of very great significance.

25. Compare Virgil, *Aen.* 5.525–8
    *namque **volans** liquidis in nubibus arsit harundo*
    *signavitque viam **flammis**, tenuisque recessit*
    consumpta in ventos: caelo ceu saepe refixa
    *transcurrunt **crinemque volantia sidera ducunt**.*
with Ovid, *Met.* 15.847–50
    (animam) lumen capere atque ignescere sensit
    *. . . . . . . : luna **volat** altius illa,*
    flami**ferumque **trahens** spatioso limite **crinem
    stella micat . . .

26. Suetonius, *Aug.* 10 *nihil convenientius ducens quam necem avunculi vindicare tuerique acta*; Cicero, *Atticus* 16.15.3 *honores patris consequi* (as Octavian's declared ambition).

27. Dio Cassius 53.4.

28. *Res Gestae* 34.

29. 12.189–194.

30. 8.731.

CHAPTER XI

1. 6.451–4.

2. Ap. Rhod. 4.1477–80.

3. 8.20–25.

4. Ap Rhod. 3.755–60.

5. 6.460; cf. Catullus 66.39 *invita, o regina, tuo de vertice cessi.*

6. 1.637 and 2.486.

7. 1.722 and 7.693.

8. 9.110 and 9.731.

9. 12.720 and *Georg.* 3.220.

10. *res rapere* was said of 'reprisals'; *vir virum legit* was said of soldiers choosing each another to be his comrade, in the formation of an army. The phrases are used with quite different values at *Aen.* 10.14 and 11.632.

11. Compare 6.190 ff. with Velleius Paterculus, 1.4 *huius classis cursum esse directum . . . columbae antecedentis volatu ferunt.*

12. See Chapter X.

13. 12.646–9, and Plutarch, *Antony* 84–5.

14. 8.589–91, and Palatine Anthology 7.670.

APPENDIX I

1. It is also relevant that Virgil early became and long remained a standard author for study in school.

2. *Corpus Inscriptionum Latinarum* 6.1779, or (a part only) *Oxford Book of Latin Verse* 352 (p. 402).

3. On the existence of such evidence see Aulus Gellius 17.10.2 *amici familiaresque P. Vergilii in his quae de ingenio moribusque eius memoriae tradiderunt* . . .

APPENDIX 2

1. The four lines are as follows:

> *Ille ego, qui quondam gracili modulatus avena*
> *carmen, et egressus silvis vicina coegi*
> *ut quamvis avido parerent arva colono,*
> *gratum opus agricolis, at nunc horrentia Martis* . . .

2. Ovid, *Tristia* 2.261; Martial 8.55.19 and 14.185.2.

3. 1.119 *arma virum*; 9.57 *arma viros*; 9.462 *in arma viros*; 9.620 *sinite arma viris*. In Book 9 the descriptions of Pandarus and Bitias (672 ff.) and of Turnus at bay (806 ff.) are said by Macrobius to echo passages in Ennius (which must themselves have echoed Homeric ones). Ennian phrases are identified by Macrobius or Servius in this same book in lines 165, 183, 422, 503, 528, 532. Norden thought that *horrisono* in line 55 and the ending *huc turbidus atque huc* in 57 were probably echoes of Ennius too.

4. See E. Brandt in *Philologus* 83(1928), where more material is adduced than has been quoted here.

5. Martial 14.186.

6. For examples of the word in this sense see Lewis and Short's Latin Dictionary, S.V. *erro*, A2 (at the end). The context here would guide the reader to the meaning required.

7. This is not to say that there are no 'difficulties' in the language, but that there is none which would be rendered less difficult by our supposing non-Virgilian authorship.

8. Some have felt that Virgil would not have made his hero even think of killing a woman, and that in sanctuary, however extraordinary the circumstances and the provocation. But objective judgement on this point is hardly possible; and the thought, if it comes to Aeneas, is anyway at once suppressed.

9. A more sophisticated discussion of the status of 2.567–88 will be found in R. G. Austin's edition of *Aeneid* 2 and his earlier article on the subject in *Classical Quarterly* N.S. 11 (1961). These ought to be consulted by any seriously interested student.

APPENDIX 4

1. The ancient MSS read *pubentesque genae* in 12.221. Some editors have preferred *tabentesque genae*, which has very little MS authority and gives no better point or more plausible picture.

APPENDIX 5

1. It has been mentioned already, but will stand repetition, that Octavian was not born into the Julian family, which claimed descent from Aeneas, but was adopted into it by his great-uncle Julius Caesar, who made him by his will his son and heir. The adopted son acquires the ancestors of his adoptive father. Similarly the younger Scipio Africanus was not a blood-descendant of the elder Scipio Africanus, but was born an Aemilius Paullus and adopted by the elder Scipio's son.

2. See D. L. Drew, *The Allegory of the Aeneid*, 1927. Only a selection of Drew's material is reviewed here.

SELECTIVE INDEX